# 100 Amazing Facts

## With Complete Proof: Celebrating Black Excellence

### A Tribute to J.A. Rogers

#### By Axsal Johnson

"The significance of African history is shown, though not overtly, in the very effort to deny anything worthy of the name of history to Africa and the African peoples."
**J.A. Rogers, World's Great Men of Color, Volume I: 1**

**An Imprint of YUSA LTD**
**www.YUSALIFE.com**
**Connect@YUSALIFE.com**
**609 Quayside Tower 252-260 Broad Street, Second Floor, Birmingham, United Kingdom, B1 2HF**

**100 Amazing Facts About The Negro: With Complete Proof**
**The 2017 Edition**
**Celebrating Black Excellence**
**A Tribute to J.A. Rogers**
**By Axsal Johnson**

Cover Art provided by: Omega_Axsal

Published In England
The Imperial Headquarters of The World.
ISBN - 978-0-9930859-7-0
Copyright ©2017 YUSALIFE

This work is dedicated to all of those who heard the call and answered...

**"Live Your Life And You Will Never Die"**

**6th Dynasty Pyramid Text**

# Contents

## Hail Up The Ancestors!

Immortality can be attained by remaining in the hearts and minds of those that we leave when we pass. We stand on the shoulders of the ancestors that created the blueprint, rose to every occasion, overcome every obstacle and remained resilient in the face of racism only to continue rising.

Whether it be through their actions, their influence, their scholarship, their attempts to unify, protect and empower Black African people all across the world. It's only right that we seek to immortalise our ancestors by learning from their mistakes, picking up from where they finished off and continuing the legacy, and that starts by saying their names! After each name, call out Asë.

Joel & Helga Rogers

Malik El Shabazz aka 'By Any Means' Malcolm X, The Honorable Marcus Mosiah Garvey, Dr Khalid 'The Black History Hitman' Mohammad, Tupac Shakur, Yaa Asantewa, Dr Yosef Ben Jocannan, Patrice Lumumba, Dr John Henrik Clarke, Noble Drew Ali. Dr Francis Cress-Wellsing, Imhotep, Tomas Sankara, Dr Amos Wilson, Martin Luther King, Queen Nzinga, Carter G Woodson, W. E. B. Du Bois, Ida B Wells, Steve Biko, Chancellor Williams, Taytul Betul, George GM James, Jean Jacques Dessalines, Ivan Van Sertima.

Darkos Howell, Alfredo Bowman Aka Dr. Sebi, Pauline Hopkins, Funimalayo Ransome-Kuti, Claudia Jones, Gustavo Vasa aka Olaudah Equiano, Bob Marley, Walter Rodney, Medgar Evers, Kwame Nkrumah, Maya Angelou, Rossa Parks, Jacob Carruthers, Na'im Akbar, Queen Nann of the Maroons, Fred Hampton, Mohammad Baba, Booker T. Washington, Frederick Douglas, Dick Gregory, Langston Hughes, John G Jackson, Audre Lorde, Toussaint Louverture, Alexandre Dumas.

Resonate in Powers (RIP) to all of the ancestors, brothers and sisters that have died during the Maafa, Slavery, Jim Crowe and the civil rights struggle. We must also take a moment to remember our brothers and sisters that have died as a result of police brutality or whilst detained in their custody whose families are likely never to receive justice.

# Asë

# Introduction

The introduction to this book serves both as a tribute and as an explanation of the importance surrounding not only this title but titles alike serving to educate and empower the Black African community in the world. In these short few opening paragraphs, I aim to give you some of the driving reasons behind working on this book although, in reality, there are more than I have the time or skill to convert into words. I also feel like it's necessary to explain why I haven't 'modernised' the title. I understand that a lot of people may feel 'Negro' is a primitive word and don't feel confident using it, maybe, even more, were put off picking up a copy.

We live in an age of information, where new discoveries and data are uncovered at a faster rate than the general population are able to process, so much so that information is going unnoticed and even becoming lost to time so to speak.

I believe like many of the teachers I have been fortunate enough to have access to through books, seminars, workshops and DVD's that we stand on the shoulders of those that passed before us and it's imperative that we celebrate and preserve their work. When I first picked up J. A. Rogers's '100 Facts,' before I'd even read it, I overstood the significance of what Rogers was trying to do, and after I finished reading, I knew exactly what I needed to do.

Rogers released this work at a period of time Black people were born to and raised by the generations first freed from slavery. For around 450 years before this, Black people had been not only removed from their homeland, stripped of their natural identity, language and culture but were then deprived of the ability to learn, and those afforded the privilege to learn were only allowed to do so to further the potential profits of their owner. So, imagine if you will, these now free people dispersed into western societies that provided little, if not any type of standard education were not able to learn about the history of their ancestors outside of the European imperial narrative.

So, what is what is the European Imperial narrative, well, in short, it's the story that was told to everyone to justify the enslavement of African people. The ridiculous notion that Europeans were on some type of godly mission to civilise the rest of the world and along with that came a range of pseudo-scientific teachings that whitewashed, replaced and refuted African Excellence. This created a delusional sense of self-righteousness, superiority and entitlement amongst the European collective that keeps itself alive by perpetuating the same misinformation that portrayed Black people as unintelligible sub-human savages.

This chronic ignorance that saw over 3,363 Black people lynched (that are recorded) just between 1882 and 1934 for reasons that can be explained as threatening the white power dynamic were all justified under the umbrella phrase Negro. In terms of political correctness, in 1934, Negro was the term widely accepted and used even amongst Black people for decades. However, due to the context of use and the current social atmosphere, it becomes attached to the negative stereotypes and so redefined and reshaped the meaning of the word.

Rogers, a learned man, knew exactly what he was doing, as presented in fact #91 that contrary to popular knowledge 'Niger,' from which the word 'Negro' derives, is not a Latin word. The word Niger found its way into Latin language becoming synonymous with 'black' as the people of the region were dark-skinned. From Niger comes 'Nigrita,' meaning 'the people of the great river,' who're known to anthropology to be part of the oldest branches of the human race.

Being an active aware and articulate African who was proud, culturally connected and now armed with information that blows the propagandised narrative wide open, Rogers made no mistake or accident in selecting his title. He published this work to stand in defiance of an effective agenda that was happy to desecrate a word that carries with it an unparalleled wealth of historical, traditional and world advancing scientific, medical, agricultural, spiritual and universal knowledge. This book would have served as a crash course to Black Excellence and achievement providing an unprecedented level of self-belief, cultural pride and should be recognised as a motivating factor behind the later civil rights movement. As far as I know, Rogers was never acknowledged or awarded respectively for the magnitude of what he did.

To understand my reasons for putting together this work, it must be acknowledged that despite the limitations of your own experience and current level of knowledge, racism was not an issue that was ended with the end of slavery, it certainly didn't end when Jim Crowe laws were abolished, nor when with integration or the rise and fall of the civil rights struggle.

The modern-day experience of racism for the Black African/Caribbean person in the western world is marginalised, and massive attempts are made to promote the illusion of equal rights and opportunity. Whereas 50 to 100 years ago the societal sentiment was aggressively more open and accepting of racism, today the tactics and methods deployed are much subtler.

Racism is very much alive, and the symptoms have only evolved to fit the current day in age, the time on plantations and building railroads may be over, but here in the West, we live in a patriarchal society that's heavily motivated by the concept of white supremacy. This agenda manifests in a variety forms such as financial institutions that create economic monopiles that deny, block and bottleneck funding into the black community to biased, outdated, non-inclusive educational systems designed to culturally disempower people of colour.

It goes beyond money and education, every society influencing institution has its objectives centred around keeping control global power, this includes religion, politics, healthcare, housing, news, entertainment, and we could go deeper if this were truly the true topic. What I hope is clear at this point is simply that racism isn't a new problem, it's not the return of an old problem but a persistent problem that we're now able to witness a lot easier because of platforms like social and televised mass media.

Comparing today, 2017, to the conditions of 1934, when Rogers first published '100 facts about the Negro,' generally speaking, Black people find themselves in a similar position, only pacified by the 'improvements' to law's that guaranty equal rights. Although time and the contents of the history pages will suggest we have come along way in 83 years, however, the continual mistreatment, miseducation and condition of the Black community tell a completely different story.

There are thousands of examples I could highlight to justify what's being said, but I think there are non-clearer than the disproportionate rates Black people are apprehended and incarcerated by the law enforcement and justice systems. In the United States, for example, Black people are roughly 13% of the overall population, but they represent around 34% of the nation's 2.2 million total prison population. And shockingly, contrary to popular belief, in England, Black people are more likely to end up in prison than in the United States when the figures are compared in proportion. 3% of the UK identify as Black, African or Caribbean but represent a staggering 12% of the prison population. So, we have literally gone from the plantation to the private prison industrial complex. *Plantation overseers and lynch-mobs to police officers, beat-cops and judges with grudges.*

*John Henrik Clarke said in Africans at the Crossroads: African World Revolution "Powerful people cannot afford to educate the people that they oppress because once you are truly educated, you will not ask for power. You will take it.*

There are a range of factors involved when it comes to assessing the state of the current educational system. What we can say for certain is that it's failing to prepare the next generations for a continually changing, digitalised global economy, a methodical approach alongside private and ivy league schooling to ensuring wealth control. More specifically, when it comes to the education of Black children, there is a clear problem. The Western schooling system is set-up to endorse a Eurocentric ideology that neglects to include the contributions to world history made by the ancestors of the students which has led to a massive negative association for many Black students and school.

Speaking from my own experience completing high school I don't remember covering any topics that provided any historical context to my Caribbean ancestry or of them achieving anything that wasn't facilitated by their previous captors. When it came to Black History month the same repetitive program that skims over the 60's, 70's and the Black inventors of the 20th century was rolled out year in year out. As if that's all there is. Conveniently, the curriculum doesn't go far back enough to talk about the vast, wealthy kingdoms of West Africa like Mali or Songhai or to the Moors of North Africa that pulled Europe from the dark ages. It must be made clear; it's not that the information isn't known to be taught, it's simply because it doesn't support the oppressive construct.

Understanding exactly what John Henrik Clarke meant when he said "Powerful people cannot afford to educate the people that they oppress," it was no shock or surprise to find out that many brothers and sisters not just in but beyond my social circles had very little interest in their culture or any type of desire to find out more about where they're from. Worse-still the connection between them and the continent was almost non-existent, this feeling of disassociation towards Africa is no accident, it's by design. The images the media project onto society about Africa show nothing but poverty, conflict and disease, so whilst our backs are turned on the continent, non-African people are buying up the land, extracting the resources and essentially bleeding it dry.

So, 83 years after the first release of '100 Amazing Facts About the Negro' much of the information is lost on our generation, which is why I felt it necessary to attempt to bring Rogers's work back to the forefront of people's minds. Our ancestors gave the world the reading, writing, mathematics, advance science, astronomy, medicine, they provided classical Greece with the blueprint which went on to be the western world. But, all that is taught is slavery and struggle. A positive reality starts with a positive mentality, and if we continue to depend on the people who benefit from our miseducation, the situation will remain the same.

### Joel Augustus Rogers – 1880 – 1966

Joel Augustus Rogers, born September 6th, 1880 in Sheffield, Westmoreland Jamaica was raised alongside 10 siblings mainly by their father Samuel John Rogers a Methodist minister and school teacher. Joel and his siblings were all able to gain a basic education and were continually reminded about the importance of education, Joel never attended university or received any formal education and thus is considered an autodidact.

After school, Joel enlisted in the British Army serving in the Royal Garrison Artillery Division based in Port Royal, a career which lasted a few short years after failing a medical exam that would have posted overseas. Like siblings, Joel decided to emigrate to the United States in 1906 and found himself briefly in Chicago Illinois before settling in New York City.

Joel's interest in the military remained as a constant throughout his life he wrote a series of articles and pamphlets that highlighted the 'African-American' experience during the American civil war of 1861-1865 and the 'African-American' experience based out of Germany in World War II.

When Joel first arrived in Chicago, he enrolled in the Chicago Institute of Arts in 1909 studying interior design supporting himself financially as a Pullman Porter during the summers. His job which he kept for around a decade allowed him to travel throughout the country and his interests in journalism & history peaked as he was able to research more about how racism, segregation and Jim Crowe laws affected the 'African-American' experience.

It was in 1917 that his first work was officially published, although done privately and printed by M.A. Donohue Co., 'From 'Superman' to Man' was a success. It was a polemic novel with a plot revolving around a Pullman Porters heated debate with a Racist Southern Politician where Rogers used a range of contemporary, historical and personal arguments to refute the notion of 'Black inferiority'. Most people consider 'From 'Superman' to Man' to be his seminal work as ideas and notions presented appear further developed and more thoroughly explored in his later publications.

In 1921, Rogers relocated to Harlem, New York City where he became acquainted and close personal friends with the 'Father of the Harlem Renaissance,' Huber Harrison who was dubbed 'The Black Socrates' by John G. Jackson. Rogers was active amongst a network of 'Street Historians' such as Carter G. Woodson, John Edwards Bruce, Arthur A. Schomburg, Marcus Garvey, and Pauline Hopkins who were responsible for the dissemination of culturally and historically empowering information for 'African-Americans'. The 'Harlem Renaissance' inspired an unprecedented sentiment of unification and nurtured a flourishing academic, artistic and intellectual spirit amongst the community.

Sadly, many of the 'Street Historians' had their scholarship denied and overlooked despite the integrity of their information on the grounds few of them were institutionally trained, segregation and the prominence of racism intensified the difficulty gaining access to library's, universities and publishing houses. Joel, like many of the rising 'Street Historians' resorted to self-publishing, writing articles for the black press, and speaking on the circuit they created for Black empowerment and liberation and maintained a self-funded career for over 50 years.

Joel's time in Harlem saw his career in journalism elevate to the mouthpiece of the Black community. He'd already established himself successfully writing for the 'Chicago Enterprise' and the 'Chicago Defender', 'Crisis,' 'American Mercury,' 'The Messenger Magazine,' 'the Negro World' and later regularly for the 'Pittsburgh Courier.' Joel also served as the Sub-editor for Garvey's 'Daily Negro Times' It was for the 'Pittsburgh Courier' that he travelled to Abyssinia (Ethiopia) to cover the coronation of Hallie Selassie which included an interview with the Emperor in 1930 and returned five years later to cover the attempted Italian occupation of Ethiopia. Joel is recognised as the only 'African-American' journalist on the ground during World War II and based on the accomplishments and reach of his writing was considered one of the top black journalists of his time.

Joel managed to publish 39 works, which in their totality alongside his physical presence played a tremendously positive role in educating, empowering and uplifting the diaspora. He articulately and unapologetically challenged institutional, systematic, academic and social racism in such a meticulously prepared, concise and understandable way he cemented himself into the blueprint that the civil rights struggle of the 60's was built on. Joel's work which still receives regular citation inspired a generation of self-supporting scholars like Dr Ben-Jochannan, John Henrike Clarke, Cheikh Anta Diop, Chancellor Williams, Amos Wilson, John G. Jackson, Ivan Van Sertima, and Molefi Kete Asante who all successfully continued the tradition of uncovering the denied African legacy and contribution to the world.

Of the 39 works (full list can be found at the back), there are some which are considered to be classics including 'World's Greatest Men and Women of African Descent,' 1935, 'The Real Facts About Ethiopia,' 1936, 'Sex and Race Vol.1-3,' 1941, 1942 & 1944 and 'Nature Knows No Colour Line: Research into the Negro Ancestry in the White Race,' 1952. Before all of the titles above were published, in 1934 Joel released the first edition of a very important 51-page book called '100 Amazing Facts About the Negro With Complete Proof: A Short Cut to the World History of the Negro' in 1934. (The 1934 edition was later revised in 1962.)

100 Amazing facts sought to showcase a present a wide variety of obscure Black Facts to empower a population of people fresh out of slavery simultaneously dealing with segregation and Jim Crowe laws. Understandably, the Black community of the 30's subject to an open and aggressive experience of racism was in need of reasons to be proud. With education for 'African-Americans' at this time being something available to the few, the narrative dictated to 'African-Americans' societally about their origins, their history, their collective achievements, their value to society, their potential and their right for self-determination was designed to keep people submissive and accepting of the mistreatment.

Irrespective of his intellectual esteem, Rogers, being a self-taught multi-lingual (German, Italian, French, and Spanish) journalist and historian who'd achieved so much in both professions, was never approached to contribute to any leading historical, anthropological research journals or projects, he was never granted or awarded any scholarships or funding grants to assist his research, he was never approached by any mainstream publishers and upon his death in the build-up to the civil rights movement, despite his success, died in debt to his book printer on March 26th, 1966. Joel's wife Helga kept the legacy alive by republishing his works up until her death in 2013.

## Quiz

Test your knowledge after reading the book, there's three different levels and all of the answers are the end of the book. Don't Cheat.

### Initiate

- Where was J. A. Rogers Born?
- What instrument did 'Blind Tom' Wiggins play?
- Who is the 'Queen of Funk'
- What country was Mansa Musa from?
- Where are there more Pyramids than anywhere else in the world?
- What is the IQ of Remani Wilfred
- What was the name of the first Black African woman in space?
- Kwame Nkrumah was the first prime minister in what country?
- What does Mikalia Ulmer make?
- Who is the father of Black History Month?

### Initiated

- How many publications did J.A. Rogers released before he passed and what is considered his seminal work?
- What country do we find the first evidence of 'mummification'?
- How many rooms are described being constructed in the ancient labyrinth?
- Who was considered the 'unique pearl of his time'?
- What are the names of NASA's human supercomputers?
- Who was the first Black Queen of England and when did she rule?
- What name is Isabel Baumfree better known as?
- Where was Patrice Lumumba from?

- Name the first Black African Women to control major publicly traded financial institute?
- Who're the fastest growing demographic in business in the United States?

## Illuminated

- What did J. A. Rogers achieve while reporting for the Pittsburgh Courier?
- What is ASCAC and who are its founders?
- What did Jordan Peel Achieve in 2017?
- How did physicians in ancient Kemet determine gender during pregnancy?
- Who brought the knowledge of smallpox inoculation to Boston in 1721?
- What did Ptah-Hotep do?
- Give three reasons Thomas Sankara is immortalised as a national and international pan-African hero.
- How many people did Robert Smalls rescue on the night of his escape?
- What is O. W Gurley responsible for founding?

# #AncestorsWork

## www.instagram.com/AncestorsWork

# The Arts & Music

1. The late Jean Michel Basquiat, Brooklyn born expressionist became the most expensive US-born artist at auction after his piece titled "Untitled" sold for £85m ($110.5m). This was the first time a painting created after 1980 had surpassed the $100m price tag and also makes him the highest selling black African artist.

2. The international music sensation Michael Jackson holds the record for the highest selling album of all time with an estimated 65m sold worldwide. It was announced by the Recording Industry Association of America (RIAA) that the late prince of pop had become the first artist to go 33 times Platinum in the United States. According to Guinness World Records, he's the most successful entertainer of all time and the only artist to have sold more than one billion records in total.

3. Quincy Jones Jr is recognised as one of the world's greatest and most successful black African figures in music; he is famed for receiving the most Grammy nominations, 79 in total and winning 27. Jones Jr, a multitalented conductor, facilitated some of largest Jazz artists, wrote songs that topped charts and was involved in the production of some of the world's most successful music, for example, Michael Jacksons 'Thriller' album lists Jones as a contributor.

4. The portrait of Americas 32nd president Franklin Delano Roosevelt that appears on the US dime was created by African artist Selma Burke.

5. Piano prodigy "Blind Tom" Wiggins, a blind, autistic savant born and sold under bondage was the 19th centuries most financially profitable entertainer.

6. Career actor, comedian, screenwriter and producer Jordan Peele made his directorial debut with his critically acclaimed box office horror 'Get Out'. The plot highlights the continually growing problem surrounding the disappearances of black African people alongside the ever-intense racial ignorance shown by unbeknown privileged Europeans. The film has been a huge success and has been acknowledged as the most profitable movie of 2017.

7. Multitalented Tylor Perry is known in the entertainment industry as the founding owner of a major Black African TV & film studios. His studio is responsible for producing over 45 films, tv shows and plays that have won a variety of awards for their success.

8. Ignatius Sancho, born aboard a slave ship in 1721 became one of the first well-known Black Britons to vote in an election. Even though in bondage he acquired an informal education and that developed his interest in the arts that would see him become a notable writer and composer. His most notable contribution was his ability to engage and fuel abolitionists as he was the first African to have his works published in England.

9. Frank Yerby, the author of 33 titles including 'The Foxes of Harrow' became the first African in America to achieve the best seller accolade in 1946. His work earned him a posthumous place in the Georgia writer's hall of fame in 2006.

10. Dubbed the 'Queen of Funk' and regularly referred to as the most 'influential female vocalist since Aretha Franklin', Chaka Khan, the highly decorated artist was heavily involved with the organisation of the Black Panther Parties free breakfast program.

**Ancient Civilisations**

11. Labelled the richest man of all time Mansa Musa Keita I, the Malian King c.1312CE -1327CE was so wealthy that on his pilgrimage to Mecca his generosity caused a 12-year economic problem for Egypt.

12. Ptahhotep, Vizer of ancient Kemet during the rule of King Djedkare Isesi is widely acknowledged as the world's first notable philosopher and author of the first book, The Maxims of Ptahhotep. The corpus of works provided instructions based on the matrilineal principles of divine universal balance and order.

13. Advanced techniques of mining have been practiced on the continent of Africa as far back as 43,000 years ago. Inhabitants of modern-day Swaziland were mining precious and semi-precious materials such as Iron Ore and Haematite. Adrian Boshier and his team discovered a haematite ore site in Lion Cavern in Swaziland where they discovered no less than 30,000 artifacts were discovered including mining tools.

14. Medical scientists of ancient Kemet developed an accurate non-intrusive method of determining gender during pregnancy. The procedure required the woman to urinate on two test sheets with emmer and barley seeds on, if the barley seed sprouted it was a boy and if the emmer sprouts it's a girl.

15. Diabetes was first identified by the physicians of ancient Kemet as early as the 1st Golden Age (c.2686BCE). Later writings compiled during the 3rd Golden Age (C. 1550BCE.) called the Ebers Papyrus contain knowledge of a wide range of illnesses along with herbal remedies attributed to Hesy-Ra. Scholars widely accept that Hesy-Ra, the High Physician serving under King Djoser as the first Dentist in history.

16. Contrary to popular belief, the first evidence of mummification is not found in Ancient Kemet (Egypt) but the lands of their westerly neighbours Libya. Uan Muhuggiag is an excavation site where the famed 'Tashwinat Mummy' was found in 1958. Testing revealed that the remains date back as far as 5600 years predating the mummies of Kemet.

17. Ile-Ife, the capital of Yorubaland in Nigeria has records that indicate that under the commission of the female ruler Ono Olowo the streets were paved, illuminated and decorated with fittings that originated in "pre-discovered" America. Evidence recovered combined with oral traditions suggest that the roads were paved from as early as 800CE.

18. The medieval kingdom of Benin was built in a scale similar to the great wall of China and is recognised by the Guinness Book of Records as "The largest earthworks in the world carried out prior to the mechanical era." The defensive walls that enclose and protected the kingdom are still partly visible in areas and were estimated to have once stretched over 10,000 miles.

19. A 3000-roomed temple complex called the 'Labyrinth' as described by Herodotus and other Greek writers were built, decorated and furnished by the people of ancient Kemet has been confirmed to exist in an area of lower Egypt called Hawara.

20. Sudan has more Pyramids than any other country. Sources indicate that there at least 220 pyramids in the Sudanese cities Gebel Barkal, Meroë Al Kurru and Nuri. Many of the Pyramids were built to serve as burial places for Kushite (Nubian) Kings, Queens, and Officials.

### Education Literacy & Intelligence

21. Russian Author, Poet and Social Activist of Ethiopian descent Alexander Pushkin, is considered the father of modern Russian language and literature and remembered as a national hero. His works were the inspiration at a period where contemporary writers published in French.

22. Mohamad Baba described as a "The Unique Pearl of his Time," the 16th-century historian and biographer is to be considered one of the greatest scholars of his day. As the author of over 60 books he contributed to the Songhai regions flourishing renaissance period, he also served as the last chancellor of the Sankore University before the invasion at a time it was considered the educational hub for the ancient world.

23. 11-year-old genius Ramarni Wilfred of Romford England received an invitation from MENSA after scoring 162 in an IQ test placing him in the top 1 percent in the UK. By eighteen months old, he was discussing news and current events and by the age for two was able to read and write competently.

24. Stephen Wiltshire, a West-Indian autistic artist, nicknamed the 'Human Camera' is famed for his impressive lifelike cityscapes rendered from memory. Some of his most famous works are the panoramas of international cities such as London and Mexico and have earned him an MBE (Member of the Most Excellent Order of the British Empire) for his contribution to British Art.

25. One of the greatest accomplishments in United States history ability to travel into space and place men on the moon. Dorothy Vaughan, Mary Jackson, and Katherine Johnson who were all employed by NASA between 1943 – 1971 made it possible for America to catch up in the 'Space Race.' Their calculations made it possible for John Glen to become the first American to make a complete orbit of the world in space on 20th February 1962 earning them the epitaph 'The human computers.'

Katherine Johnson, the navigational specialist, was awarded the presidential medal of freedom in 2015 Barrack Obama in recognition of her achievements and accomplishments.

Dorothy Vaughan is recognised as the first Black woman to head a department at NACA (National Advisory Committee for Aeronautics) in 1949, and Mary Jackson fought to become NASA's first Black female aerospace engineer.

26. Ernie Davies the American Football prodigy was the first Black winner of the Heisman Trophy in 1962 for his fantastic contribution to college sports and becoming a number 1 NFL draft pick. Sadly, despite his relentless courage and persistence he lost his battle with Leukemia and his professional career never materialised.

Davies, during the period of the civil rights movement, a time when universities and educational institutes did not typically offer financial assistance to black athletic students, Davies was offered as many as 50 scholarships proposals.

## Exploration

27. 38-year-old Nigerian pilot Ademola Odujinrin became the first African to fly solo around the world. He flew a Cirrus SR22 single-engine aircraft and pit-stopped on five different continents landing in 15 different countries.

28. Historical records indicate that two large fleets of Malian sailors led by Mansa Abubakari II arrived in America 1311CE, 181 years before the expedition led by European Christopher Columbus.

29. At age 24 in 2007, Barrington Irving Jr, C.D. became the youngest person to pilot a plane around the world solo also making him the first black person and first Jamaican to accomplish this feat.

30. Dr. Mae C. Jeminson was as the first African woman in space as part of NASA's Endeavour mission in 1992. Her role was the onboard physician and during the 190 hours in space conducted experiments on motion sickness and weightlessness.

31. On May 19, 2006, at 7 a.m. battling with symptoms of bronchitis, frostbite and the elements of nature, Sophia Danesburg became the first Black African woman to climb Mt Everest, the world's biggest mountain.

32. Cuban born Arnaldo Tamayo Mendez who graduated from the Cuban Air Force and selected to fly in the Soviet Union's Intercosmos mission to space on September 18th, 1980, made him the first Cuban and person African descent to enter space.

### Science & Invention

33. On May, 9th 1899, John A. Burr was awarded U.S. Patent number 624,749 for his rotary blade that revolutionised manual lawn mowing. His blade was designed to avoid becoming clogged up with clippings which were some common time-consuming problems of obsolete lawnmowers. Burr died at the age of 78 from influenza with over 30 patents revolving around lawn care and agricultural inventions to his name.

34. 24-year-old Arthur Zang, Cameroonian engineer invented Cardiopad, a lifesaving innovative heart-scanning diagnostics tablet providing rural residents of Africa remote access to cardiologists to review their results. Testing has been conducted and verified by the Cameroonian Medical community wielding accuracy results as high as 97.5%.

35. The self-taught engineer Gerald A. Lawson is the developer of the Fairchild Channel F, the first home gaming console that had interchangeable cartridges, an innovation that paved the way for consoles such as the Sega Mega Drive, PlayStation, and Xbox.

36. Electrical Engineer and computer graphic designer Marc Regis Hannah was the principle developer responsible for developing the computer systems that produced special effects for many of the blockbuster hits such as Jurassic Park, Aladdin, Beauty & the Beast and his technology was used in Terminator 2. Hannah was one of the six founding partners of SGI (Silicon Graphics, Inc) in 1982 a company that has contributed to the progression of filmmaking.

37. After returning from service in world war I, entrepreneur and inventor Frederick McKinley Jones was granted his first patent in 1939 for creating a machine that gave the correct change with tickets. A mechanic by day and the towns projectionist at the silent movie theatres by evening, Jones created a cost-effective sound synchronisation machine to help the theatre industry upgrade to play motion pictures with audio.

   Jones most notable contribution was inventing and making the refrigerated vehicle work so that food and other perishables could be transported without spoiling. This proved a vital breakthrough for the transport of blood that saved thousands of lives during world war II.

38. Theoretical physicist Dr Shirley Ann Jackson is a truly phenomenal woman of the 21st century she became the first Black woman to graduate from Massachusetts Institute of Technology (MIT) with a doctorate in physics in 1973. Jackson's breakthrough research enabled others to successfully invent the portable fax, the touch-tone telephone, solar cells, fibre optic cables, and the technology behind caller ID and call waiting.

Jackson currently serves as the president of Rensselaer Polytechnic Institute, the oldest technological research university in the United States and is the highest paid president of a privately-owned college. Since 2014, Jackson has sat on the Presidents Intelligence Advisory Board, awarded the National Medal of Science, the nation's greatest honour for contributions in the fields of science and engineering by President Obama in 2015 and has been awarded an astounding 53 honorary degrees from various institutes across the world.

39. In 1962 James West, co-invented the Electret microphone and developed the transducer technology that is still in 90% of microphone technology to this very day. West's technology has become the industry standard and is used in the manufacturing of things from recording microphones used in studios down to tape recorders, baby monitors, and hearing aids, it's estimated that over 2 billion products are made each year including his technology. West, as well as being introduced into the National Inventors Hall of Fame he has over 40 U.S. patents and over 200 international patents.

40. Ludwick Marishane became Africa's youngest patent filer in the year in 2007 at the age of 17 with his product DryBath. DryBath is a gel that replaces water, soap, and lotion which enables people in areas where water is scarce to bathe. Marishane was awarded and celebrated as 1 of 12 of the brightest minds & best student entrepreneurs of 2011. Marishane is also regarded by Time magazine as one of the 30 under 30's changing the world.

41. Garret Morgan could be regarded as one of the 20th centuries biggest heroes responsible for preserving millions of lives with his invention of the 'Safety Hood' which provided the blueprint for modern-day gas masks.

"Unable to sell his gas mask to fire departments in the South, Morgan hired an actor friend to pose as an inventor while he dressed up as an Indian chief. The actor would announce that Big Chief Mason would go inside a smoke-filled tent for ten minutes. When Morgan emerged after 25 minutes unharmed, people were amazed. Business boomed."

Morgan was alive at the turn of the century when cars were becoming common and in he witnessed a traffic incident at an intersection that prompted him to invent a traffic control device and file for a patent in 1922. Patent number 1,475,024 was awarded in 1923 for his three position traffic signals.

## Medicine

42. Henrietta Lacks died of cervical cancer at the age of 31 in 1951, the medical legacy that she unknowingly left behind has been responsible for saving millions of lives. The samples taken from Henrietta without her knowledge have been described as 'the most important cells in medical research' and still provide valuable data to this day. The abnormalities in the cells were named HeLa after the first two initials of her name by George Otto Gey who cultured them.

The HeLa cells have been pivotal in medical breakthroughs throughout the last 60 years, for example, in 1954 Jonas Salk used the cells to develop the polio vaccine. This created a increases demand for the cells, the requirement was met, and samples were sent all across the world to support the research into cancer, AIDS, radiation, and countless medical pursuits. Lack's cells were the first ever to be cloned successfully and since the 1950's over 20 tonnes of her cells have been grown for experimentation.

43. At the age of 14, 9th-grade student Tony Hansbury Jr II developed a safer, more effective and less complicated method of sewing up hysterectomy patients that proved to be 3x faster than previous techniques.

44. Percy Lavon Julian is regarded as one of the world's most influential chemists who overcome various race-based boundaries to secure more than 130 chemical patents. Many of his patents were the result of the pioneering innovations in chemical synthesis from plants one such example was the product he created called physostigmine used in the treatment of glaucoma. His research and work helped set out the blueprint for the steroid drug industry's production of cortisone, other corticosteroids, and birth control pills.

In 1953, Julian Laboratories was founded, and he went on to recruit many of the best chemists that he'd worked with previously at Gidden, their first major contract was to the value of 2 Million dollars (16 Million in 2017) to provide progesterone. His consistent success and breakthroughs with his work in the private sector helped reduce the cost of steroid drugs making them more available. By 1961, before selling the company for 2.3 Million dollars, the chemists at Julian Labs had developed methods that quadrupled their yield, reducing their product cost from $4,000 per KG to $400 per KG.

45. Mary Seacole, Jamaican born businesswoman, and healer tops the 'Greatest Black Britons' list for her role in the Crimean War as a Nurse and spirit raiser of wounded Soldiers despite the continual struggles she faced because of the colour of her skin. The War Office denied Seacole's offer to assist, and so she took it upon herself, at her own expense to travel to the conflict zone where she established a hotel as her base of operations. For the soldiers that she comes into contact with and helped, she became known as 'Mother Seacole.'

46. Malaria claims the life of a child every 30 seconds and around 1 million people die from the disease each year making it one of the largest killers in the world. 90% of malaria cases occur in Sub-Sahara Africa and has

inspired Dr. Valentin Agon to research and develop a plant-based anti-malarial medication called Api-Palu to combat the disease. The product unanimously won 2016's IFA (Innovation Prize for Africa) top prize of $100,000 which will increase the production rates and increase the availability. Testing has proven that Dr. Agon's Api-Palu is more efficient and more cost-effective than previous methods.

47. The oldest medical texts in the world defining aliments, illnesses, diseases, medicines and surgical procedures all date and originate back to ancient Kemet. There are nine main texts named after European owners (Edwin Smith, Chester Beaty, Carlsburg), sites of discovery (Kahoun, Ramesseum), cities they're presently housed in (Leyden, London, Berlin) or the editor (Ebers).

The oldest of the collection is the Kahoun Papyri which dates to circa 1950BCE; it contains three sections, one dealing with human medicine, the other on veterinary science and the last on mathematics.

The Edwin Smith Papyrus dates to circa 1600BCE and is the only surviving copy of an ancient Kemetic trauma surgery textbook. The content is thought to be based on texts that existed at least 1000 years before it and consists of 22 pages covering 28 cases of trauma physically examined, diagnosed, treated and analysed.

48. Charles R. Drew is the pioneering researcher and practicing surgeon that smashed through the race-based obstructions during the 'Segregation years' to become one of the most important medical scientists of the 20th

century. Drew is responsible for breakthroughs in the preservation of blood plasma and consequently saved thousands of lives during the second world war. He was also responsible for implementing the standards for the process of long-term blood banking.

49. Otis Boykin, the multifaceted electrical engineer, and inventor, had an amazingly diverse career. He is most notably known for his inventions that revolutionised pacemakers making them more effective. But, most people don't know that when he died, he had 26 recognised patents including technology used in radio's and television and a resistor that became in high demand for military missile systems.

50. Historically speaking, Smallpox ranks as one of the fatalist diseases of all time with figures suggesting that 300 million people died in the 20th century alone. The documented smallpox outbreak in Boston 1721, which infected roughly 11,000 residents could have been even worse if it had it have not been for the advanced knowledge of smallpox inoculation shared by an enslaved African man named Onesimus.

A Puritan congregation purchased Onesimus in 1706 led by Cotton Mather an honorary member of the London Royal Society. In letters sent to LRS, Mather revealed that he was shown the method of inoculation by Onesimus who had the scar on his arm as proof. Although Onesimus was directly responsible for the rise in survival rates in Boston, he remained in bondage.

### Politics

51. Bernie Grant, British Guiana born politician dedicated just short of 4 decades of his life to his community campaigning and fighting for racial equality & justice. He had a successful career as a politician serving as a local councillor in the Borough of Haringey after his election in 1985. He also became the first African in Britain at the head of a local authority which was responsible for the welfare of a quarter of a million people. Bernie ranked 9th in the 'Greatest Black Britons' list.

52. Ellen Johnson-Sirleaf was elected the 24th president of Libera and is the first woman to hold this position in an African country and has done for 12

years. Aged 78, Ellen shall be retiring from office in October 2017 after the Liberian election. Johnson-Sirleaf was a huge proponent of women's rights and won the Nobel Peace Prize alongside fellow Liberian Leymah Gbowee and Tawakkol Karman of Yemen in 2011 for their "for their non-violent struggle for the safety of women and women's rights to full participation in peace-building work."

53. Samora Moises Machel was instrumental in the liberation of Mozambique from Portuguese colonial rule in 1975 by leading the FREMELIO (Frente de Libertação de Moçambique) and becoming the first president of independent Mozambique.

Machel died in 1986 under suspicious circumstances in a plane crash that claimed the lives of 35 people. A memorial took place, and a monument was erected at the Mbuzini crash site in 1999 at the expense of the South African government.

54. Olaudah Equiano or Gustavus Vassa as he was known in his living life is widely regarded and considered as Black Britain's political founding father. A freed slave whose autobiography detailing the endurances of Africans published in 1789 became central to the abolishment movement in Britain and heavily influenced the Slave Trade Act of 1807 that ended slavery in Britain and its colonies.

Olaudah was taught to read and trade and did so on behalf of his owners. By the age of 22, he was able to purchase his freedom from his owner Robert King for the sum of £40 which today would equate to around

£6000. Olaudah would go on to become a successful merchant eventually becoming a social activist with the more time that he spent in England.

55. Diane Abbot became the first black woman to be elected to the British Parliament, and she was elected to Westminster city council before winning the Hackney North and Stoke Newington constituency for the Labour Party in 1987. She was elected along with Paul Boateng and Bernie Grant who became the first black men to be elected to the British Parliament. All three were voted into the 'Greatest Black Britons' list, Diane ranked 29th, Paul 47th & Bernie 9th.

### Rulers & Leaders

56. Queen Philipa was the daughter of William III of Hainault (modern-day Belgium) who was married to England's King Edwards III making her the first known Black Queen of England in 1328. Of the 14 children she had, the eldest and most historically notable was Edward the Black Prince' who was an accredited military leader.

Queen Phillipa also ranked 5th on the 'Greatest Black Britons' list for her service in the absence of King Edward, its documented she served as regent multiple times and earned the love from the citizens for her compassion and even convinced the king to have mercy on Burghers of Calais.

57. Taytu Betul was the Ruling Queen & Counter-Part of King Menelik II Negus Negast, and together they were the saviors of Ethiopian independence and inspiration for Africa's continental liberation. During the Italian attempt to colonise Ethiopia, Taytu and Menelik galvanised the people to defend the land and said no to foreign conquest.

In the historic treaty of Wuchale (1889) her suspicions of the Europeans intentions were proved correct when she tore up a document in the Italians faces after spotting intentional mistakes that would have saw her country become a protectorate state of Italy.

Taytu was a highly educated, diligent, compassionate warrior queen known for riding into battle alongside her king and is the attributed founder of Addis Abba the current capital of Ethiopia.

58. Queen Charlotte Sophia is recognised as the second Black Queen of England (1761-1801), and the first Black Queen of the United Kingdom of Great Britain and Ireland from 1801 until her death in 1818. Her tenure lasted 57 years and 70 days making her the longest-serving British consort to date.

    Charlotte was a Queen for the people; she funded the first and longest standing maternity care institute in London now named Queen Charlotte's and Chelsea Hospital to help improve the birth rate.

59. Queen Nanny is regarded as a national hero throughout the Caribbean and particularly in Jamaica for her role as a spiritual and military leader of the Maroons. Maroon means runaway and refers to the Africans that fled plantations to form a community that opposed slavery and British colonial rule.

    Nanny was of the Ashanti people and was enslaved during the 18th century before escaping with other enslaved Africans to the mountainous east areas of the island in Portland and St. Thomas.

    Nanny was documented to be around the age of 60 at the peak of her tenure in control of the Windward Maroons, and her cunning guerrilla military tactics were said to surprise and overwhelm the British soldiers that attempted to apprehend them.

60. Thomas Sankara in his four years tenure as the President of Burkina Faso proved to be one of the most forward-thinking leaders of an African nation in post-colonial history. Sankara, of military background, rose to political power after a coupe and was elected head of state and by August 4th, 1984, the same day he changed the countries name from the Republic of Upper Volta to Burkino Faso.

He has been immortalised as a national Hero for his endeavours to improve the country which involved inoculating over 2.5 million children in less than a week, improving the countries literacy rate from 13% in 1983 to 73% in 1987 and also planted over 10 million trees to combat desertification. The countries wheat production doubled through the redistribution of land, and over 350 communities were encouraged to build local schools and medical dispensaries with their own labour.

Sankara played a significant role in the fight for women's rights condemning genital mutilation, forced marriages and removed patriarchal barriers that obstructed women in the workplace and even elevated women to senior positions in the government.

61. Kwame Nkrumah became Africa's first continental born head of state when he was elected Prime Minister in 1951 despite being in custody of the retiring British colonial regime. Nkrumah became the motor that drove Ghana towards its independence which was finally won on March 6th, 1957.

Nkrumah dedicated his life to the decolonisation of Africa, and his Pan-African political policies began to take form after being exposed to the teachings of Marcus Garvey. While studying for his Anthropology PhD at the London School of Economics, Nkrumah was instrumental in organising the 5th Pan-African Congress in Manchester which hosted 90 delegates including honoured figures such as Jomo Kenyatta, C.L.R James. W.E.B Dubois and Hastings Banda.

62. Meroe was the capital of the Kingdom of Kush (Nubia aka modern-day Sudan) which preceded, existed alongside and outlasted the empire of Kemet. Sources from contemporary writers exist that speak highly of the line of African Warrior Queens they called Candaces. The title was Europeanised from Ktde or Kenteke meaning Queen Mother. There are five uncontestably known Kenteke, Shanakdakhete 177 BCE–155 BCE, Amanirenas 40 BCE–10 BCE, Amanishakheto 10 BCE–1 CE, Amanitore, 1–20 CE. and Amanikhatashan 62–85 CE

    Aminirenias goes down in history as the most prolific of the Kenteke during her rule, to the north, Egypt was a Roman province under Emperor August Caesar. She gave the order to march her 30,000-strong army to Aswan, driving out the Romans and destroying roman monuments. Roman prefect, Publius Petronius retaliated ruthlessly and attacked Kushite cities, he captured Qasr Ibrim in 23BCE and attacked into the territory as far as Napata.

    Aminirenias managed to escape capture and ordered that the garrison built by the Romans be attacked. The surviving records show a standoff, terms were agreed, and the Romans withdrew their forces declaring 'Pax Romana' and returned up north.

63. Gaspar Yanga (c.1545), remembered as the 'first liberator of the Americas,' led the most successful slave-uprising in colonial Mexico and established a self-sustaining maroon community that resisted decades of Spanish attacks that became officially recognised as a free black settlement.

    Yanga organised guerrilla forces called 'Palenque's that raided Spanish-Mexican settlements for resources and eventually became the colonial Spaniards biggest problem. In 1609 Spanish authorities sent a squadron of well-armed mercenaries who were defeated by the surprise tactics and superior knowledge of the terrain. Although victorious, Yanga's settlement was destroyed, and they evaded capture until 1618 after years of negotiations San Lorenzo de Los Negros now known as Yanga after its founder was officially recognised as a free state.

64. During the 10th century, seafaring North Africans were known to the "British Isles" and are recorded making their way there via Iberia and assimilating with local societies even holding positions of governance. One such example is Niger Val Dubh, also recognised by history as Kenneth the Niger, King of Scotland reigning from 962CE to 967CE. Not much is known about the legacy of Kenneth, he had one son, Kenneth III who didn't content for the throne after his father's death.

65. Patrice Lumumba considered one of the modern martyrs of Pan-Africanism and advocates total African independence and liberation was the first democratically elected prime minister of the Democratic Republic of Congo.

On January 30th, 1960, at the Independence Day ceremony attended by King Baudouin of the Belgians the ex-colonial leader and members of the international press. Lumumba delivered an impromptu speech reminding his fellow Congolese nationals that independence wasn't handed to them and it came with a fight, which placed a target on his back and bolstered his status as a political threat to the Belgians.

A coupe faction assassinated Patrice Lumumba under the influence of both American and Belgian officials. Lumumba was killed by a firing squad alongside Maurice Mpolo and Joseph Okito on January 17th, 1961.

66. Robert Smalls of South Carolina was born into slavery and performed the unimaginable task of sailing a heavily armed confederate warship through occupied hostile waters freeing himself and 17 passengers including his own family from slavery.

In the twilight hours of May 13th, 1862, Smalls assumed the position of captain mimicking the absent white General Ripley navigating the ship through various checkpoints even offering the right naval signals at five confederate blockades.

Smalls was dubbed a hero in the north and became an advocate for Black enrolment into the Union Army and was said to be responsible for the recruitment of 5,000 soldiers. He returned to active duty in the Union Army part of the Admiral Du Pont's South Atlantic Blockading Squadron and was eventually promoted to captain in December 1863 making him one of the highest paid African soldiers of the war. This was because the current captain hid during the heat of battle and Smalls stepped up and secured the victory.

## Sports

67. Walker Smith Jr, better known as Sugar Ray Robinson is remembered as the greatest pound for pound boxer of all time. During his amateur stage, his record was 85-0 (wins-losses) with 69 wins coming by knock-out, 40 of them in the first round. Over his 25-year professional career which ended in 1965, he clocked out leaving a record of 173-19-6-2 (wins-losses-draws-no contests) with 108 knockouts in 200 professional bouts, ranking him among the all-time leaders in knockouts.

From the years 1943 to 1951 he went an unbeaten run of 91 fights which is the third longest streak in boxing history. Sugar Ray Robinson is best remembered for his achievement being the first boxer to win five divisional titles.

Two years after his retirement in 1965, he was inducted into the International Boxing Hall of Fame and later in 1984; The Ring magazine placed Robinson No. 1 in its book "The 100 Greatest Boxers of All Time."

68. At the Mexico City Summer Olympics 1968, Jim Hines became the first person to run 100 meters under 10 seconds with a time of 9.95, a record he held for 15 years.

69. Usain Bolt, until paralleled is known as the world's fastest man and worlds most successful sprinter of all time. He holds world records in the 100m (9.58s), 200m (19.19s) and the 4X100m relay (36.84s) a record he shares with his countrymen Yohan Blake, Michael Frater & Nesta Carter.

   Bolt accumulated 28 Gold medals over his professional career and is the only sprinter to achieve the 'triple-triple' by winning three Olympic golds at three consecutive Olympic games. Bolt's 9 Golds have since been reduced to 8 since Nesta Carter failed a prohibited substance test.

70. Serena & Venus Williams two sisters from Compton California have dominated women's tennis since the 1990's accumulating a total of 14 Grand Slam titles playing as a pair in the doubles competition. In Singles, they have 30 Grand Slam titles between them, Venus has 7, and in January, Serena became the first player male or female to achieve 23 Grand Slam Major titles.

71. Ibtihaj Muhammad broke down cultural boundaries at the Rio Olympics in 2016 by becoming the first American to compete wearing a hijab. Muhammad secured the first medal for the females fencing team when she won bronze in the Sabre category.

72. In 2016 August 2016 at the Rio Olympic Games, Simone Manuel became the first Black women to win an Olympic Gold medal in the swimming pool

when she came joint first with Canadian Penny Oleksiak clocking a record-breaking time of 52.70 seconds in the 100m freestyle.

73. Brazilian international football sensation and revelation Edson Arantes do Nascimento also known as Pele is recognised as the most successful striker in football history. In his 21-year professional career, he scored a record 1,279 goals in 1,363 games with 21.5% of his goals being scored in three's making him the record holding hattrick scorer.

   Pele still holds the records after 58 years and 15 tournaments for being the youngest hat-trick scorer (17 years and 244 days) and youngest scorer in a final (17 years and 249 days) in the world cup competition. Pele is also the only player to have won the World Cup on three occasions and scored 77 competitive goals for Brazil.

74. Francis Morgan Ayodélé "Daley" Thompson the English former decathlete who holds four world records in the competition, two Olympic Gold Medals from 1980 and 1984 and multiple world and European championship wins become the first athlete, in any event, to hold an Olympic, World, Continental and Commonwealth in a single event concurrently.

75. Wilma Rudolf overcome multiple childhood illnesses such as pneumonia, scarlet fever, polio and even wore a brace until the age of 8 to become the world's fastest women in the 60's. Rudolf was also the first American women to win three Olympic Gold Medals in both track and field during the 1960 games in Rome.

Upon her return home to Tennessee after becoming an international star hailed as the then fastest woman in history, Rudolf refused to attend her own homecoming celebration because of the segregation laws. Her refusal to participate resorted in her banquet becoming the first integrated event in Charlestown Tennessee. She continued to take part in protests until the segregation laws were completely abolished.

76. Charles Haley, the versatile defensive end athlete, was the first NFL football player to win 5 Super Bowl rings (years 1989, 1990, 1993, 1994 & 1996). Haley was only recently joined on that pedestal by Tom Brady who has five rings playing for the same team.

77. Gymnast sensation Simone Biles the is widely accepted as the greatest gymnast of all time male or female. Biles holds the record for the most Olympic single golds as part of an incredible 19 Olympic and world titles making her the most decorated in the United States.

**Warfare**

78. The Ahosi warriors also known by their Europeanised moniker the 'Dahomey Amazons' were an all-female Benin based platoon used in the fight against French colonial invasion. Originally formed by King Houegbudja as an Elephant hunting and herding group it was not until the rule of King Agaja in 1708CE that the group was militarised into the Kings guard.

At times, the Ahosi made up as much as one-third of the total army. Women joined freely, and records indicate that girls enrolled as young as eight years old. The last known surviving sister of the Ahosi, named Nawi, died in 1979 and claimed to have fought against the French in 1892.

79. During the Second World War (1 Sep 1939 – 2 Sep 1945) until 1942 the U.S Marine corps was an exclusively white branch of the military until the demand for soldiers called for increased. Recruitment began for Black Marines on June 1st and were trained under segregation laws in Monteford Point and by 1949 20,000 Marines had been trained.

Despite the intentions to fight for the same country, Black trainee marines were subjected to racism as their NCO's (non-commissioned officers) where southern white supporters of segregation. By January 1943, Edgar R. Huff became the first Black NCO, and in February, Gilbert H. Johnson a 19 army and navy veteran became the first Black drill instructor.

300 of the still living 20,000 veterans were belatedly recognised and awarded with Congressional Gold Medals for their fight for the right to fight and achievements on Friday 17th, 2012.

80. After a terrible accident on a bomb recovery operation, surgeons were forced to amputate Carl Brashear's left leg below the knee. Brashear refused to accept verdicts given by naval medical boards that were trying to retire him and underwent an inspirational rehabilitation. Brashear proved that he was still able to dive and perform his tasks and carried on serving as a clearance and salvage diver and in 1970 Brashear qualified as U.S History's first Black Master Diver.

## Miscellaneous

81. In 1994, the Fédération Internationale des Échecs or World Chess Federation (FIDE), awarded Maurice Ashley the Grandmaster title in 1999 making him the first Jamaican Chess Grandmaster.

82. Trinidad born journalist and Anchor, Trevor McDonald, most known for 'News at Ten' was awarded a knighthood in 1999 for his services to international and British journalism. McDonald also ranked number 7 on the Great Black Britons list.

83. The Association for the Study of Classical African Civilisations formally known as ASCAC was founded in 1984 by Drs. John Henrik Clark, Asa Grant Hilliard, Leonard Jeffries, Jacob H. Carruthers, Rkhty Amen, Yosef Ben-Jochannan, and Maulana Karenga.

    ASCAC focuses on disseminating a continually evolving body of knowledge that rescues, reconstructs, and restores African history and culture for the improvement of the global worldview of ancient and modern Africa.

84. O. W. Gurley, an affluent educator, landowner and former appointee of the president Grover Cleveland is known as the father of 'Black Wall Street.' Gurley purchased 40 acres he named Greenwood during the Oklahoma land rush of 1889 with the intentions of only selling the land to Black people and also provided a safe-haven to Black people fleeing from southern oppression.

    By 1913, the heavy regulation of Oklahoma's segregation laws allowed the growing Greenwood district to blossom. At its peak there was a population of over 15,000 people and 600 businesses including practitioners of law and medicine, schools including Dunbar and Booker T. Washington schools, Vernon AME Church which still stands today, Restaurants, Theatres, Grocery Stores, Hotels, and a range of haberdasheries, drug stores, cafes, barbershops and beauty salons.

The economy in Greenwood was so strong the Black dollar circulated the community 36 to 100 times before entering a white pocket, the average income of a household exceeded the minimum wage of today and most impressively at a time where Oklahoma only had two airports, between the residents of Greenwood there were 6 aeroplanes.

The brutal end of Black Wall Street came with Americas worst act of domestic terrorism to date, spearheaded by the Ku Klux Klan, a pack of white Europeans the Greenwood district to the ground. Over the course of 12 hours on June 1st, 1921, 300 people lost their lives and 1,256 homes destroyed displacing over 3,000 people, ironically the black family-owned planes were used against the residents to drop explosives making Tulsa Race Riots the first time a bomb was dropped aggressively on American Ground.

The High court judged that Black people began the riot and so no justice or compensation was awarded for the loss of life, business, or property. Hurley was someone who lost out massively, and his wealth was wiped out immediately, and records show a loss of $200,000 ($2.5 million today.)

85. Considered the 'Father of Black History Month', Carter G Woodson was born in New Canton, Virginia to former-enslaved parents in 1875. Growing up he was soon recognised as an exceptional student and went on to become one of the first Black Africans to earn a doctorate from Harvard University in 1912.

Woodson devoted his life to establish a nationwide curriculum highlighting African contributions to civilisation, it began with 'Negro History Week' in February 1926, and by 1976 it had become so popular it was expanded to the entire month. February was chosen to honour the birthdays of the abolitionists of his time Frederick Douglas and Abraham Lincoln.

Woodson was also responsible for the founding of some key organisations and associations pivotal in the upliftment and re-education of Black African people such as Association for the Study of Negro Life and History in 1915. He also founded The Journal of African American History in 1916 and wrote many historical works, essays and publications most notably 'The Miseducation of the Negro' in 1933.

86. Nigerian born Godwin Ajala will be forever be remembered as a U.S. national hero for his actions during the tragic events that unfolded on September 11th, 2011 when the two towers of the World Trade Centre were attacked. Ajala, a qualified Nigerian Lawyer, immigrated to America and was working as a security guard while training part-time for the New York Bar exam, he was last seen helping people escaping the building. Godwin was the only Nigerian listed among the 3000+ fatalities.

87. 13th Century warrior princess Yennenga is known as the 'Mother of the Mossi' people hailing out of modern-day Burkino Faso. Yennengas legend survives mainly through oral tradition, and the story tells us that she was the daughter of King Nedega of the Dagomba region of Modern day Ghana. As well as being a beauty admired by many she was a well-trained warrior equal to the skill of the best-trained soldiers in the army.

There are various accounts of the story, and one such example is when she came of age her father refused to allow her to marry, she planted a field of wheat which Yannenga let grow and rot without cropping the yield as a message to her father to express how she felt. The message was ignored by her father causing her to run away.

Yennenga fled north eventually meeting and marrying a man of the Bissa (or Mande) people. They named their son Ouedraogo who was sent to be raised by Yennengas father, when Ouedraogo was of age he returned to defeat his father's people (Bissa or Mande). The marriages between Ouedraogo's army and the Bissa or Mande people created the people we now call the Mossi.

88. The social media hashtag 'Black Girl Magic' that celebrates the revolutionary rise of the natural, beautiful, creative, self-empowered Black women has been studied and quantified in economic terms. According to Nielson, the global information, data collection and measurement institute, Black women are the most influential group on the planet in the areas of fashion, music, entertainment and self-care. The report called 'African-American Women: Our Science, Her Magic' analyses the spending, watching, listening and eating habits and concluded that Black women are the driving force behind the total Black spending power which is estimated to reach $1.3 trillion by 2021.

89. During a period in modern British history when news media gave very little coverage to problems issues, Jamaican born Val McCalla founded the Voice magazine in 1982 which went on to become the mouthpiece of Black news in Britain and Europe's largest Black magazine. Val grew the publication and in 8 years was selling 53,000 copies a week making considerable profits from the recruitment advertisement pages. For his work and service providing the black community with a platform to air their voice, McCalla was voted number 68 in the 100 Great Black Britons list.

90. Isabell Baumfree, born into slavery in New York circa 1797, more commonly remembered as Sojourner Truth the self-liberated African activist who campaigned for the abolition of slavery and women's rights was the first African to take the European to court in America and successfully win the case.

Truth, who'd been converted to Christianity dedicated her life to campaigning against the mistreatment of Africans in America and especially for female rights. Her most famed moment was the speech that she delivered in Akron, Ohio at the Women's Rights Convention known as 'Ain't I A Woman?'.

Although technically illiterate, she was intelligent and perfectly able to articulate herself, she also met Abraham Lincoln and narrated her memoirs which were transcribed by her friend Olive Gilbert who had them published by Lloyd Garrison in 1850.

91. During the violent civil rights period of the sixties and seventies 30-year-old Bobbie Seal and 24-year-old Huey P. Newton united together to form the Black Panther Party for Self-Defence. Created in response to the increasing public brutality of white oppression and systematic racism the BPP as a political organisation outlined their objectives and goals in a 10-point program which included rights to freedom, land, housing, employment and education.

The original members in addition to Seale & Newton were: Elbert "Big Man" Howard, Sherman Forte, Reggie Forte and Little Bobby Hutton. The organisation fundamentally focused on self-reliance, preservation and defence and set up 35 community-based 'survival' projects that benefited the people. Once such project which was the most successful of them all, the 'Children's free breakfast program' which at its height provided 20,000 breakfasts to disenfranchised children.

Due to their ability to unify and organise masses of oppressed people prepared to protect themselves lawfully, the BPP was labelled as a terrorist organisation and called "the greatest threat to the internal security of the country" by FBI director J Edgar Hoover.

92. Bob Johnson self-made success and co-founder of Black Entertainment Television (B.E.T) became the first African in America to become a billionaire in 2001 after selling a cable channel to Viacom for 3 Billion Dollars.

    After a divorce from his wife Sheila who was also a co-founder of B.E.T his fortune dropped, and he exited the Forbes billionaire list. He spent time investing his money and rebuilt his wealth becoming the first Black person to hold majority ownership shares in a basketball team and re-entering the Forbes list in 2007.

93. After being stung twice at the age of 4, Mikaila Ulmer became fascinated with bee's and their contribution to the eco-system and was encouraged to enter a local lemonade making competition. Using a family recipe sent by her Grandmother, Mikaila decided to use honey to sweeten the drink and 'Me & The Bee's Lemonade' was born.

    Since her small-town success, Mikaila's business has grown and gone national, and her lemonade has been taken on by 55 U.S Wholefoods stores in a multi-million deal.

94. Born to former slaves in July 1864, Maggie Lena Walker went on to become a prominent teacher, activist and businesswoman and in 1902 became the first woman of any race in America to charter a bank, 'The St. Luke Penny Savings Bank'. Walker went on to agree to be the chairman of the board when the bank merged with two other local banks serving the community as a black-owned financial institute.

95. Suzanne Shank is the first Black African in America to lead and control a major financial institution that is traded on the open market and is one of the most powerful women on Wall Street. Shank, now with the nickname 'Trillion Woman' because she's CEO of two trillion-dollar firms (Siebert Brandford Shank & Co. LLC and Siebert Financial Corporation) has overseen trillions of dollars' worth of financial contracts.

96. In February 2014, internationally known pop and R&B entertainer Aliaune Damala Badara Thiam, better known as Akon, publicly announced the launch of his renewable solar power company with the goal of providing electricity to 600 million Africans in rural areas.

    By late 2017, the Akon Lights Africa project was operating in over 15 different countries, in 480 communities providing electricity to 80 million Africans, a figure that is increasing day to day.

© David Monfort – dagency.fr

97. After his death on May 19th, 1875 newspaper obituaries called Jeremiah G Hamilton 'The Richest Black Man in the United States.' Hamilton worked in and around Wall Street for about 40 years at a time when it was totally dominated by whites and accumulated an estimated wealth of 2 Million Dollars which equates to around $43 Million today.

    Hamilton was a controversial figure, he was said to buy policies on ships that he would purposely sink, and despite being well known in his time even receiving regular press coverage, Hamilton is widely forgotten by history.

98. Madam C.J Walker is remembered in history as being the first self-made female millionaire of any race in the United States. Walker, born Sarah

Breedlove created specialist products promoted to assist rapid hair growth after losing her hair as a result of a scalp condition. Walker travelled around the country delivering product demonstrations and training sales beauticians who became known as 'The Walker Agents' each making anything between $5 and $15 per day making her very popular amongst the Black community.

As well as being a successful entrepreneur, Walker also involved herself in the civil rights struggle and funded various projects for the community's benefit including the NAACP, and she even restored Fredrick Douglas's home. She was also part of a delegation that travelled to the White House campaigning to make lynching a federal crime.

99. As per the 'Forbes Rich List' released in March 2017, there are a total of 2,043 billionaires in the world 10 of them are Black with a combined wealth of 44 Billion dollars.

1. #105  – Aliko Dangote           – 13.1 Billion
2. #147  – Mohammed Al-Amoudi      – 10.1 Billion
3. #338  – Mike Adenuga            – 5.3 Billion
4. #612  – Isabel dos Santos       – 3.5 Billion
5. #651  – Robert Smith            – 3.3 Billion
6. #748  – Oprah Winfrey           – 3.0 Billion
7. #1137 – Patrice Motsepe         – 1.8 Billion
8. #1520 – Folorunsho Alakija      – 1.5 Billion
9. #1729 – Michael Jordan          – 1.3 Billion
10. #1901 – Mohammed Ibrahim        – 1.1 Billion

100. Multiple reports conducted over the last decade indicate that Black Women in America are the fastest growing demographic in the entrepreneurial business sector with a total growth of 322% between 1997 and 2015. The growth of Black female-owned businesses between the years 2007 and 2016 was 112% which was over double the 45% growth from all the other groups combined.

As of 2016, women-owned 38% of all businesses in America with Black women owning 44% of them employing over 375,000 people and generating more than $51.4 million. It's also a fact that Black women in America now hold 61% majority of all Black-owned businesses.

# The Arts & Music

1. "On Thursday, May 18, art market history was made as Basquiat's Untitled, 1982 was sold for a record-breaking $110.5 million at Sotheby's Contemporary Art Evening sale. The price made this work the highest paid at auction for a work by an American artist and for any artwork created after 1980. It is the sixth most expensive work ever sold at auction and only ten other works have broken the $100 million mark."

www.sothebysinstitute.com/news-and-events/news/basquiat-bonanza/

"Born in Brooklyn, New York in 1960 to a Haitian father and a mother of Puerto Rican descent, Basquiat's racial blackness impacted him throughout his entire life. He encountered racism and racial stereotyping in the neighbourhoods in which he grew up, in the schools, he attended, in the popular culture around him, in the New York club scene he was so close to, and, most significantly, in the 1980s art world that largely embraced him."

**P.3 Performing blackness at the heart of whiteness: The life and art of Jean-Michel Basquiat by Christopher f. Johnston – August 2008**

2. An article published by Billboard on 02/06/2017 stated "The Recording Industry Association of America (RIAA) has certified the set at 33-times platinum in the U.S., extending Thriller's record as the highest certified album in history.

That means Thriller -- released in 1982 -- has earned 33 million equivalent album units in the U.S. That sum blends traditional album sales (one album sale equals one unit), tracks sold from an album (10 tracks sold equals one unit) and on-demand audio and/or video streams (1,500 streams equals one unit).

www.billboard.com/articles/news/7693419/michael-jackson-thriller-highest-certified-album

The 65m album sales are the official record according to the book of Guinness World Records.

**Martin Gitlin, (March 1, 2011). The Baby Boomer Encyclopaedia. ABC-CLIO. p. 196. ISBN 978-0-313-38218-5. Retrieved March 15, 2012.**

According to both the book of Guinness World Records and The World Record Academy "His awards include multiple Guinness World Records (eight in 2006 alone), 13 Grammy Awards, 13 number one singles in his solo career — more than any other male artist in the Hot 100 era — and the sale of over 750 million records worldwide, making him the world's Most Successful Entertainer of All Time."

www.worldrecordacademy.com/entertainment/most_successful_entert ainer_of_all_time-Michael_Jackson_sets_world_record%20_90258.htm

3. Born March 14 1933, Chicago Illinois, Quincy Delightt Jones, Jr. Widely recognised as the greatest producer of all time, nominated for a record 79 Grammys and won more Grammys than any living musician (27); produced the best-selling album of all-time (Michael Jackson's Thriller) & the best-selling single of all-time (We Are the World); produced, composed, conducted, arranged or performed on more than 400 albums; and responsible for scoring over 30 theatrical movies. Quincy Jones production discography. (2017, May Wikipedia, The Free Encyclopedia. Retrieved 12:20, August 10, 2017 from:

https://en.wikipedia.org/w/index.php?title=Quincy_Jones_production_ discography&oldid=782560499

4. "The source of Roosevelt's image on the dime has recently received much attention. John R. Sinnock, the chief engraver at the U.S. Mint, has his initials on the profile. The dime's head, however, is merely a mirror image of the plaque created by Selma Burke, with the exception of a few detail changes in the arrangement of Roosevelt's hair. Moreover, the National Archives and Records Administration of the Franklin D. Roosevelt Library in Hyde Park, New York, stated that the dime portrait originated with the sculpture of Franklin Delano Roosevelt done by Selma Burke."

www.encyclopedia.com/people/history/historians-miscellaneous-biographies/selma-burke

5. Bethune hired out "Blind Tom" Wiggins from the age of eight years to concert promoter Perry Oliver, who toured him extensively in the US, performing as often as four times a day and earning Oliver and Bethune up to $100,000 a year, an enormous sum for the time, "equivalent to $1.5

million/year [in 2004], making Blind Tom undoubtedly the nineteenth century's most highly compensated pianist"

https://en.wikipedia.org/wiki/Blind_Tom_Wiggins
"The Battle of Manassas", Art of the States (on line) Archived March 4, 2010, at the Wayback Machine.
Henry Louis Gates; Evelyn Brooks Higginbotham (2004). African American Lives. Oxford University Press. p. 85. ISBN 0-19-516024-X.

6. Time.com reported on 08/08/2017 that "Jordan Peele's 'Get Out' Is the Most Profitable Film of 2017…. Get Out, the low-budget comedy-horror film that explores racism in America, has enjoyed a whopping 630% return on investment, more than any other movie released in 2017."

http://time.com/money/4891175/get-out-jordan-peele-most-profitable-movie-2017/

Get Out grossed $175.5 million in the United States and Canada and $77 million in other territories for a worldwide gross of $252.4 million, against a production budget of $4.5 million. "Get Out (2017)". Box Office Mojo.

http://www.boxofficemojo.com/movies/?page=daily&id=blumhouse2.htm

7. Georgia Encyclopaedia entry concerning Tyler Perry reads: "Tyler Perry, an Atlanta-based writer, producer, and performer, is one of the most commercially successful African American filmmakers in history. Tyler Perry Studios, which opened in Atlanta in 2008, is the first major film studio in the nation to be owned by an African American."

http://www.georgiaencyclopedia.org/articles/arts-culture/tyler-perry-b-1969

As a result of the collective releases from Tylor Perry Studio's they have collected over 50 different accolades including 21 NAACP Image awards, 4 AAFCA Awards and BET Best movie.

http://tylerperry.com/tyler/awards/

8. "The first African prose writer whose work was published in England… He died in 1780, and two years later his Letters were published, proving that 'an untutored African may possess abilities equal to a European'. His work

attracted over 1,200 subscribers. 'Let it no longer be said', wrote one reviewer, 'by half informed philosophers, and superficial investigators of human nature, that Negers, as they are vulgarly called, are inferior to any white nation in mental abilities'."

**www.100greatblackbritons.com/bios/ignatious_sancho.html**

9. For the complete list of Yerby's work
   **https://en.wikipedia.org/wiki/Frank_Yerby#Novels**
   **Valerie Frazier, (July 16, 2002). "Frank Yerby (1916-1991)". New Georgia Encyclopaedia..**

10. "Born Yvette Marie Stevens, March 23, 1953, in Great Lakes, IL; given the name Chaka Adunne Adufle Yemoja Hodarhu Karifi by an African priest, c. 1969... Khan became active in the black power movement, joining the Black Panther Party and working with the organization's free breakfast program for children..."

    **www.encyclopedia.com/people/literature-and-arts/music-popular-and-jazz-biographies/chaka-khan**

    Awards: Numerous Grammy awards, including two with Rufus for best R&B performance by a duo or group, for "Tell Me Something Good" and "Ain't Nobody"; for solo work, including best female vocalist and best vocal arrangement, 1983, for "Bebop Medley," best R&B single by a female vocalist, 1984, for "I Feel For You," and best R&B vocal performance, female, 1993, for "The Woman I Am"; honored by International Association of African-American Music for career excellence, 1992.

    **www.biography.com/people/chaka-khan-262761**

### Ancient Civilisations

11. "Mūsā I of Mali, Mūsā also spelled Musa or Mousa, also called Kankan Mūsā or Mansa Musa (died 1332/37?), mansa (emperor) of the West African empire of Mali from 1307 (or 1312). Mansa Mūsā left a realm notable for its extent and riches—he built the Great Mosque at Timbuktu—but he is best remembered in the Middle East and Europe for

the splendour of his pilgrimage to Mecca (1324). The historian al-'Umarī, who visited Cairo 12 years after the emperor's visit, found the inhabitants of this city, with a population estimated at one million, still singing the praises of Mansa Mūsā. So lavish was the emperor in his spending that he flooded the Cairo market with gold, thereby causing such a decline in its value that the market some 12 years later had still not fully recovered." **Encyclopædia Britannica, inc. Article Title: Musa I of Mali Contributor: John Coleman de Graft-Johnson**

Time magazine & Business Insider both place Mansa Musa at the top of the list of the wealthiest people of all time.
**http://time.com/money/3977798/the-10-richest-people-of-all-time/**
**http://www.businessinsider.com/richest-people-in-history-2010-8?IR=T**

"The list uses the annual 2199.6 per cent rate of inflation to adjust historic fortunes – a formula that means $100 million in 1913 would be equal to £2.299.63 billion today... Mansa Musa I ruled West Africa's Malian Empire in the early 1300s, making his fortune by exploiting his country's salt and gold production... In comparison, the poorest man on the list (**http://www.independent.co.uk/news/world/world-history/meet-mansa-musa-i-of-mali-the-richest-human-being-in-all-history-8213453.html**) is 82-year-old Warren Buffett, who at his peak net worth, before he started giving his fortune to charity, was $64billion.

12. Reported by the Chicago Tribune: Sunday, July 2nd 1893 "The Oldest Book In The World, It's not the Bible, As so many think.."

**http://archives.chicagotribune.com/1893/07/02/page/27/article/oldest-book-in-the-world**

"The oldest work of philosophy known to us is the "Instructions of Ptahhotep" which apparently goes back to 2880 B.C. 2300 years before Confucius, Socrates and Buddha. Ptahhotep was Governor of Memphis, and Prime Minister to the King, under the Fifth Dynasty. Retiring from office, he decided to leave to his son a manual of everlasting wisdom. It was transcribed as an antique classic by some scholars prior to the Eighteenth Dynasty."

**William Durant The Story of Civilization: Our Oriental History ch. VIII EGYPT p. 193**

13. Ngwenya Mine is situated on the north-western border of Swaziland. Its iron ore deposits constitute one of the oldest geological formations in the world, and also have the distinction of being the site of the world's earliest mining activity.
Deposits at Ngwenya were worked at least 42 000 years BP (Before Present) for the extraction of red haematite and specularite (sparkling ores).

http://whc.unesco.org/en/tentativelists/5421/

Reported by South African archaeologists have reported discovering the world's oldest mine. The mine, in an iron-ore mountain in neigh boring Swaziland, is 43,000 years old, according to radio carbon dating.
It was discovered by Adrian Boshier, field research officer for the Museum of Man and Science in Johannesburg. Mr. Boshier made his discovery at Bomvu Ridge In the Ngwenya (Crocodile) mountain range in Swaziland. - 43,000-Year-Old Mine Discovered in Swaziland, Special To The New York Times FEB. 8, 1970

**Africa: Mother of Western Civilization – Dr Yosef Ben-Jochannan p.56-
http://bit.ly/2vy9lqa**

14. **Bob Breir – Everyday lives of the Egyptians. P.235**

15. "Diabetes was one of the first diseases described, with an Egyptian manuscript from c. 1500 BCE mentioning "too great emptying of the urine". The Ebers papyrus includes a recommendation for a drink to be taken in such cases."

**Jacob Roberts, (2015). "Sickening sweet". Distillations. 1 (4): 12–15**

Excavations on Hesy-Ra's tomb provide evidence that show he was serving under the rule of King Djoser as pointed out by Wolfgang Helck in 'Geschichte des alten Ägypten (= Handbuch der Orientalistik. Abt. 1: Der Nahe und der Mittlere Osten. Bd. 1: Ägyptologie; Abschnitt 3). BRILL, Leiden 1968, page 47.
Among the many titles attributed to Hesy-Ra were:
Great one of the dentists (Egyptian: Wer-ibeh-senjw) & Magician of Mehit (Egyptian: Hem-heka-Mehit). Hesy-Ra would be the very first person in Egyptian history to be officially entitled as an occupational dentist

Dilwyn Jones: An Index of ancient Egyptian titles, epithets and phrases of the Old Kingdom, Volume 1 (= BAR international Series, vol. 866, section 1). Archaeopress p. 381, no. 1412.

16. "The most noteworthy find at Uan Muhuggiag is the well-preserved mummy of a young boy of approximately 2 1/2 years old...The boy's organs were removed, as evidenced by incisions in his stomach and thorax, and an organic preservative was inserted to stop his body from decomposing... Radiocarbon dating determined the age of the mummy to be approximately 5600 years old, which makes it about 1000 years older than the earliest previously recorded mummy in ancient Egypt.

    https://en.wikipedia.org/wiki/Uan_Muhuggiag

    In 1958-1959, an archaeological expedition led by Antonio Ascenzi conducted anthropological, radiological, histological and chemical analyses on the Uan Muhuggiag mummy. The specimen was determined to be that of a 30-month old child of uncertain sex, who possessed Negroid features. **V. Giuffra; et al. (2010). "Antonio Ascenzi (1915-2000), a Pathologist devoted to Anthropology and Paleopathology" (PDF). Pathologica. 102: 1–5.**

17. Department of the Arts of Africa, Oceania, and the Americas. "Ife Pre-Pavement and Pavement Era (800–1000 A.D.)." In Heilbrunn Timeline of Art History. New York: The Metropolitan Museum of Art, 2000

    http://www.metmuseum.org/toah/hd/pave/hd_pave.htm (October 2001

    Movements, Borders, and Identities in Africa edited by Toyin Falola, Aribidesi Adisa Usman - **http://bit.ly/2fgnfaf**

18. **Guinness Book of World Records 1974:** - "The largest earthworks in the world carried out prior to the mechanical era were the Linear Earth Boundaries of the Benin Empire (i.e. Benin city in the Mid-Western State of Nigeria.) They were the first reported (by modern European scholars) in 1903CE and partially surveyed in 1976CE.

The mediaeval Nigerian city of Benin was built to "a scale comparable with the Great Wall of China". There was a vast system of defensive walling to-talling 10,000 miles in all.

http://www.whenweruled.com/?p=18

19. Lost labyrinth of Egypt scanned: The Mataha-expedition researched the lost labyrinth of Egypt at Hawara. A colossal temple described by many classic authors like Herodotus and Strabo, to contain 3000 rooms full of hieroglyphs and paintings. A legendary building lost for 2 millenia under the ancient sands of Egypt. Bringing the highest level of technology to unlock the secrets of the past. The sand of Hawara was scanned in 2008 by the Belgian Egyptian expedition team. Although ground penetrating techniques are used by archaeologists for years, the Mataha-expedition (Mataha = labyrinth in Arabic) was the first to apply this technology at Hawara, to solve the enigma born in the Renaissance for once.

**Mataha Expedition Hawara 2008, NRIAG - Ghent University/Kunst-Zicht A project coordinated by Louis De Cordier www.labyrinthofegypt.com**

20. "While pyramids are associated with Egypt, the nation of Sudan has 220 extant pyramids, the most numerous in the world." - Pollard, Lawrence (2004-09-09). "Sudan's past uncovered"

**http://news.bbc.co.uk/1/hi/world/africa/3641516.stm**

Nubian pyramids were constructed (roughly 240 of them) at three sites in Sudan to serve as tombs for the kings and queens of Napata and Meroë. The pyramids of Kush, also known as Nubian Pyramids, have different characteristics than the pyramids of Egypt. The Nubian pyramids were constructed at a steeper angle than Egyptian ones. Pyramids were still being built in Sudan as late as 300 AD.

**https://en.wikipedia.org/wiki/Pyramid#Sudan**
Also see: 'Nubian Pyramids'
**https://en.wikipedia.org/wiki/Nubian_pyramids**

21. By far the most famous of all the Blacks in Russian history, however, was Alexander Sergeievich Pushkin–patriarch of Russian literature. Born in Moscow on May 26, 1799, Pushkin was descended on his mother's side from Major-General Ibrahim Petrovich Hannibal–an Ethiopian prince who became a favourite of Tsar Peter I (1682-1725)... Pushkin has been positively identified as the father of Russian literature, and composed in the Russian language at a time when most Russian intellectuals were writing in French. Of Pushkin, Feodor Dostoevsky wrote that, "No Russian writer was ever so intimately at one with the Russian people as Pushkin."

https://tseday.wordpress.com/2008/08/24/alexander-pushkin-russias-greatest-black-poet/

22. "When the [Songhai] Empire collapsed, due to an Arab and European invasion in 1591 AD, its intelligentsia were arrested by the conquerors and dragged in chains across the Sahara. One of these scholars was Professor Ahmed Baba. The author of 60 books, Professor Baba enjoyed a very high reputation. Amongst the Songhai, he was known as "The Unique Pearl of his Time". In a Moroccan text from the period, the praise for him was even more gushing. He is described as "the imam, the erudite, the high-minded, the eminent among scholars, Abu l-Abbas Ahmed Baba..."

Professor Ahmed Baba of Songhai: Greatest scholar of the sixteenth century world. http://www.whenweruled.com/?p=64

"By the end of Mansa Musa's reign (early 14th century CE), the Sankoré Masjid had been converted into a fully staffed Madrassa (Islamic school or in this case university) with the largest collections of books in Africa since the Library of Alexandria. The level of learning at Timbuktu's Sankoré University was superior to that of many other Islamic centers in the world. The Sankoré Masjid was capable of housing 25,000 students and had one of the largest libraries in the world with between 400,000 to 700,000 manuscripts."

See Said Hamdun & Noël King (edds.), Ibn Battuta in Black Africa. London 1975, pp. 52-53.

23. Black To The Future: IQ Higher Than Einstein's "11-Year-Old" Ramarni Wilfred Asked To Join Mensa - **Reported by Romford Recorder, Published: 07:00 09 May 2014 by Hayley Anderson**

24. Taken from Stephen Wiltshire's Official Website's Biography Page: **www.stephenwiltshire.co.uk/biography.aspx**

   Stephen Wiltshire is an artist who draws and paints detailed cityscapes. He has a particular talent for drawing lifelike, accurate representations of cities, sometimes after having only observed them briefly. He was awarded an MBE for services to the art world in 2006. Stephen was born in London, United Kingdom to West Indian parents on 24th April, 1974. As a child he was mute, and did not relate to other people. Aged three, he was diagnosed as autistic. He had no language and lived entirely in his own world.

25. See: 'Who Are The Hidden Figures?' written by Kerry Kolbe 26 January 2017 in conjunction with the producers of the Film 'Hidden Figures'

   **www.telegraph.co.uk/films/hidden-figures/the-women-who-inspired-the-film/**

26. For Ernie Davis's Full Biography see: **www.biography.com/people/ernie-davis-9267805**

## Exploration

27. Nigeria's Odujinrin becomes first African to fly solo around the world **www.vanguardngr.com/2017/04/nigerias-odujinrin-becomes-first-african-fly-solo-around-world/**

28. Acclaimed Black British Scholar nicknamed 'The Black History Man' ascertains in his work 'When We Ruled *2nd Edition -1 Oct 2014' as excerpted on his website,

   Malian sailors got to America in 1311 AD, 181 years before Columbus. An Egyptian scholar, Ibn Fadl Al-Umari, published on this sometime around 1342. In the tenth chapter of his book, there is an account of two large maritime voyages ordered by the predecessor of Mansa Musa, a king who inherited the Malian throne in 1312. This mariner king is not named by Al-Umari, but modern writers identify him as Mansa Abubakari II.

**http://www.whenweruled.com/articles.php?lng=en&pg=5**

29. For Barrington Irving Jr, C.D. Full Biography see:
**www.nationalgeographic.com/explorers/bios/barrington-irving/**

30. For Dr. Mae C. Jeminson's Full Biography see:
**www.biography.com/people/mae-c-jemison-9542378**

31. "In 2006 Sophia Danenberg became the first African American and first black woman from anywhere in the world to climb the highest mountain in the world, Mount Everest in the Himalayas (Nepal)... In the spring of 2006, at age 34, with one week of planning, Sophia Danenberg began the climb of Mount Everest in the Nepal, the highest mountain in the world at 29,000 feet. Danenberg, along with eight people, signed up for an "unguided" climb which gave her the help of two Sherpas, weather reports, food, and oxygen. Danenberg carried her own gear and pitched her own tent. She had no guide on the climb to make decisions for her. On May 19, 2006, after two months climbing, she and her party reached the summit of Mount Everest."
**www.blackpast.org/aah/danenberg-sophia-1972**

32. Arnaldo Tamayo Méndez, (born Jan. 29, 1942, Guantánamo, Cuba), Cuban pilot and cosmonaut, the first Latin American, the first person of African descent, and the first Cuban to fly in space.

For Arnold's full biography see: **www.britannica.com/biography/Arnaldo-Tamayo-Mendez**

## Science & Invention

33. Archived by **www.thoughtco.com/green-lawns-john-albert-burr-4072195** 'The Innovation of John Albert Burr: Black American Inventor Improves Rotary Lawn Mower.'

For U.S. Patent see: **www.google.com/patents/US624749**

34. As reported by Forbes on Feb 9, 2012 @ 02:22 'Young African Invents Touch Screen Medical Tablet' - Here's an example of African innovation at its finest.

Arthur Zang, a 24 year-old Cameroonian engineer, has invented the Cardiopad, a touch screen medical tablet that enables heart examinations such as the electrocardiogram (ECG) to be performed at remote, rural locations while the results of the test are transferred wirelessly to specialists who can interpret them. The device spares African patients living in remote areas the trouble of having to travel to urban centers to seek medical examinations.

According to Zang, the Cardiopad is "the first fully touch screen medical tablet made in Cameroon and in Africa." He believes it is an invention that could save numerous human lives, and says the reliability of the pad device is as high as 97.5%. Zang says he invented the device in order to facilitate the treatment of patients with heart disease across Cameroon and the rest of Africa. So far, several medical tests have been carried out with the Cardiopad which have been validated by the Cameroonian scientific community.

www.forbes.com/sites/mfonobongnsehe/2012/02/09/young-african-invents-touch-screen-medical-tablet/#75fd82fa7055

35. Jerry Lawson, a self-taught engineer, gave us video game cartridges: "If you've got fond memories of blowing into video game cartridges, you've got Gerald "Jerry" Lawson to thank. As the head of engineering and marketing for Fairchild Semiconductor's gaming outfit in the mid-'70s, Lawson developed the first home gaming console that utilized interchangeable cartridges, the Fairchild Channel F. That system never saw the heights of popularity of consoles from Atari, Nintendo and Sega, but it was a significant step forward for the entire gaming industry. Prior to the Channel F, games like Pong were built directly into their hardware -- there was no swapping them out to play something else -- and few believed that you could even give a console a microprocessor of its own. Lawson, who passed away at 70 from diabetes complications in 2011, was the first major African-American figure in the game industry. And, just like the tech world today, it still isn't as diverse as it should be.

59

Only 2 percent of game developers in 2005 were African-American, according to a study by the International Game Developer Association (who also honored Lawson as a game pioneer a month before his death).

www.engadget.com/2015/02/20/jerry-lawson-game-pioneer/

36. Electrical engineer and computer graphics designer Marc Regis Hannah was born on October 13, 1956, in Chicago, Illinois to Huber and Edith Hannah. He attended the Illinois Institute of Technology, with funding from a scholarship awarded by AT&T's Bell Laboratories. Hannah received his B.S. degree in electrical engineering in 1977 before going on to Stanford University where he obtained his M.S. degree in 1978 and his Ph.D. degree in 1985.

www.engadget.com/2015/02/20/jerry-lawson-game-pioneer/

In 1982, Hannah co-founded Silicon Graphics, Inc. (SGI) with Jim Clark and five others, a company that went on to be well-known for its computer graphics technology. In 1986, he was named the company's principal scientist for the creation of computer programs like Personal IRIS, Indigo, Indigo2, and Indy graphics that were used to create effects for movies like Jurassic Park, Aladdin, Beauty and the Beast, The Hunt for Red October, and Field of Dreams. George Lucas' Industrial Light & Magic used Silicon Graphics' technology to create Terminator 2. Hannah's programs have also been used to create television commercials and the opening introduction for Monday Night Football. In addition, the company's technology was used in engineering, research, and for military applications. Hannah is a partial owner of Rondeau Bay, a construction company in Oakland, California.

For full biography visit: www.encyclopedia.com/education/news-wires-white-papers-and-books/hannah-marc-1956

37. Frederick Jones was an inventor best known for the development of refrigeration equipment used to transport food and blood during World War II.

For his full bio see: www.biography.com/people/frederick-jones-21329957

38. The Honorable Shirley Ann Jackson, PhD became the 18th president of Rensselaer Polytechnic Institute on July 1, 1999. Dr Jackson is a theoretical physicist. Since coming to Rensselaer, Dr Jackson has led the development of the Rensselaer Plan (the Institute's strategic blueprint), has begun implementation of much of the Plan, while restructuring processes and procedures; and secured a $360 million unrestricted gift commitment to the university.

www.nytimes.com/ref/college/faculty/coll_pres_jacksonbio.html

She followed this interest to the Massachusetts Institute of Technology (MIT) where she received a bachelor, and doctoral degree, all in the field of physics. In doing so, she became the first African-American woman to earn a PhD from MIT.

Jackson conducted successful experiments in theoretical physics and used her knowledge of physics to foster advances in telecommunications research while working at Bell Laboratories. Dr Jackson conducted breakthrough basic scientific research that enabled others to invent the portable fax, the touch-tone telephone, solar cells, fibre optic cables, and the technology behind caller ID and call waiting.

www.black-inventor.com/Dr-Shirley-Jackson.asp

For Dr.Shirley Ann Jackson's full biography see:
http://president.rpi.edu/president-biography

39. James West is a U.S. inventor and professor who, in 1962, developed the electret transducer technology later used in 90 percent of contemporary microphones.

For his full bio see: www.biography.com/people/james-west-538802

"It's estimated that over 90 percent of the microphones in use today are electret mics, and more than 2 billion of these devices are produced worldwide every year... He holds more than 40 US and over 200 international patents. He has been inducted into the National Inventors Hall of Fame and the National Academy of Engineering."
https://arstechnica.co.uk/information-technology/2016/05/electret-microphone-james-west-bell-labs/

40. Garret Morgan: The Safety Hood "Morgan's biggest venture was his safety hood. As a young man, he had seen firefighters struggling to withstand the suffocating smoke they encountered in the line of duty. In 1914 Morgan secured a patent for his device, a canvas hood with two tubes. Part of the device held on the back filtered smoke outward, while cooling the air inside. Morgan's safety hood won accolades and wide adoption in the North, where over 500 cities bought it, over time. He sold the hoods to the U.S. Navy, and the Army used them in World War I. But sales in the segregated South proved challenging. Morgan's hood got great press in 1916, when he used it to save workers in a collapsed tunnel under Lake Erie. But Cleveland's newspapers and city officials wrote Morgan -- who had ventured into the tunnel first -- out of the story, lauding other men and ignoring Morgan's heroism. It would take years for the city to recognize his contributions. Morgan died in 1963, vindicated as a hero of the Lake Erie rescue and restored to his place in history."
**http://www.pbs.org/wgbh/theymadeamerica/whomade/morgan_hi.ht ml**

The first American-made automobiles were introduced to consumers just before the turn of the twentieth century, and pedestrians, bicycles, animal-drawn wagons and motor vehicles all had to share the same roads. To deal with the growing problem of traffic accidents, a number of versions of traffic signaling devices began to be developed, starting around 1913. Morgan had witnessed a serious accident at an intersection, and he filed a patent for traffic control device in 1922. In 1923, the US Patent Office granted Patent No. 1,475,024to Garrett Morgan for his three-position traffic signal.

**https://en.wikipedia.org/wiki/Garrett_Morgan**

For Traffic Signal U.S. Patent see:
**https://www.google.com/patents/US1475024**


### Medicine

41. "Born from humble beginnings in Limpopo, Marishane has been crowned as innovator par excellence and one of the 12 brightest minds and best student entrepreneur in the world by Google in 2011. Today he is taking his company, Headboy Industries, and his DryBath brand to new heights...

His innovative invention, a Bath-Substituting gel called DryBath (a type of gel that people can use to clean themselves), is designed to replace the need for soap, water and skin lotion. At age 17, Marishane claimed the proud title of inventor and became South Africa's youngest patent filer. Today he holds a Bachelor of Business Science, majoring in Finance and Accounting, from the University of Cape Town. In December 2013, TIME Magazine named him as one of the 30 people, under 30, who are changing the world -- one of only two Africans on the list. DryBath is designed to provide more hygiene to two billion people without adequate water access, who still use the traditional bucket-bathing method."

TED Speaker Biography - Ludwick Marishane - **www.ted.com/profiles/300214**

42. Henrietta Lacks (born Loretta Pleasant; August 1, 1920 – October 4, 1951) was an African American woman whose cancer cells were the source of the HeLa cell line, the first immortalized cell line and one of the most important cell lines in medical research. An immortalized cell line will reproduce indefinitely under specific conditions, and the HeLa cell line continues to be a source of invaluable medical data to the present day."

**Sarah Zielinski, "Cracking the Code of the Human Genome. Henrietta Lacks' 'Immortal' Cells". Smithsonian.**

Lacks was the unwitting source of these cells from a tumor biopsied during treatment for cervical cancer at Johns Hopkins Hospital in Baltimore, Maryland, U.S. in 1951. These cells were then cultured by George Otto Gey who created the cell line known as HeLa, which is still used for medical research.

**Denise Grady, (2010-02-01). "A Lasting Gift to Medicine That Wasn't Really a Gift". The New York Times.**

The ability to rapidly reproduce HeLa cells in a laboratory setting has led to many important breakthroughs in biomedical research. For example, by 1954, Jonas Salk was using HeLa cells in his research to develop the polio vaccine.

**Van Smith, (2002-04-17). "Wonder Woman: The Life, Death, and Life After Death of Henrietta Lacks, Unwitting Heroine of Modern Medical Science". Baltimore City Paper**

HeLa cells were in high demand and put into mass production. They were mailed to scientists around the globe for "research into cancer, AIDS, the effects of radiation and toxic substances, gene mapping, and countless other scientific pursuits". HeLa cells were the first human cells successfully cloned in 1955, and have since been used to test human sensitivity to tape, glue, cosmetics, and many other products. Since the 1950s, scientists have grown 20 tons of her cells, and there are almost 11,000 patents involving HeLa cells.

Denise Watson Batts, (2010-05-10). "Cancer cells killed Henrietta Lacks – then made her immortal". The Virginian-Pilot. pp. 1, 12–14. Retrieved 2012-08-19. Note: Some sources report her birthday as August 2, 1920, vs. August 1, 1920.

For a full biography uncovering the life of Henrietta Lacks see title: **The Immortal Life of Henrieta Lacks – Rebecca Skloot**

43. Tony Hansbury II, 14-Year-old developer of the nicknamed 'Hansbury Stitch', the innovative time saving technique of sewing up hysterectomy patients featured in CNN's 2014 article: "These 8 whiz kids are the future of medicine."
http://edition.cnn.com/2014/08/14/health/8-whiz-kids-future-medicine/index.html

For the full story see: **http://jacksonville.com/news/2009-04-22/story/14-year-old_surgeon_to_present_findings_today**

44. Percy Lavon Julian (April 11, 1899 – April 19, 1975) was an African American research chemist and a pioneer in the chemical synthesis of medicinal drugs from plants. He was the first to synthesize the natural product physostigmine and a pioneer in the industrial large-scale chemical synthesis of the human hormones progesterone and testosterone from plant sterols such as stigmasterol and sitosterol. His work laid the foundation for the steroid drug industry's production of cortisone, other corticosteroids, and birth control pills.

He later started his own company to synthesize steroid intermediates from the wild Mexican yam. His work helped greatly reduce the cost of steroid intermediates to large multinational pharmaceutical companies, helping to significantly expand the use of several important drugs.

Julian received more than 130 chemical patents. He was one of the first African Americans to receive a doctorate in chemistry. He was the first African-American chemist inducted into the National Academy of Sciences, and the second African-American scientist inducted (behind David Blackwell) from any field.

In 1953, Julian founded his own research firm, Julian Laboratories, Inc. He brought many of his best chemists, including African-Americans and women, from Glidden to his own company. Julian won a contract to provide Upjohn with $2 million worth of progesterone (equivalent to $16 million today).

Julian Laboratories chemists found a way to quadruple the yield on a product on which they were barely breaking even. Julian reduced their price for the product from $4,000 per kg to $400 per kg.[5] He sold the company in 1961 for $2.3 million (equivalent to $18 million today).[27] The U.S. and Mexico facilities were purchased by Smith Kline, and Julian's chemical plant in Guatemala was purchased by Upjohn.

In 1964, Julian founded Julian Associates and Julian Research Institute, which he managed for the rest of his life.

**https://en.wikipedia.org/wiki/Percy_Lavon_Julian**

For Percy Lavon Julian's full biography see:
**www.biography.com/people/percy-julian-9359018**

45. 1.) Mary Seacole Nurse in the Crimean war, 2.) Wilfred Wood First black bishop 3.) Mary Prince First black female author to be published, 4.) Olaudah Equiano Political activist & 5.) Queen Phillipa Wife of Edward III" - Nurse is greatest Black Briton - As reported by the Guardian, Tuesday 10 February 2004, full article: **www.theguardian.com/uk/2004/feb/10/britishidentity.artsandhumaniti es**

"Mary Seacole's reputation after the Crimean War (1853-1856) rivalled Florence Nightingale's. Unlike Nightingale, Seacole also had the challenge to have her skills put to proper use in spite of her being black. A born healer and a woman of driving energy, she overcame official indifference and prejudice. She got herself out to the war by her own efforts and at her own expense; risked her life to bring comfort to the wounded and dying soldiers; and became the first black woman to make her mark on British public life. But while Florence Nightingale has gone down in history and become a legend, Mary Seacole was relegated to obscurity until recently."

http://www.100greatblackbritons.com/bios/mary_seacole.html

She was widely known to the British Army as "Mother Seacole"
http://www.100greatblackbritons.com/bios/mary_seacole.html

46. Malaria statistics via UNICHEF:
www.unicef.org/health/files/health_africamalaria.pdf

Dr Valentin Agon reported by Forbes: "A ground-breaking anti-malarial drug made from natural plant extracts has won the 2016 Innovation Prize for Africa… Api-Palu, made by Dr Valentin Agon of Benin, won the IPA $100,000 grand prize in Gaborone, Botswana… Agon's medication, Api-Palu, is both significantly cheaper than mainstream pharmaceutical anti-malarial drugs, and more effective, the IPA said in choosing him as the winner. "It has great inhibitory effects on 3D7 strains of plasmodium falciparum the causative agent of malaria," the judges said. It is available in Benin, Burkina Faso, Tchad, and Central African Republic (CAR); while Agon says he intends using the prize money to increase production, and be in every country in Africa by 2017.

For the full article see:
https://www.forbes.com/sites/tobyshapshak/2016/06/23/malaria-hivaids-solutions-win-big-at-innovation-prize-for-africa/#21e0d659779a

47. Excerpts taken from **Magic and Medical Science in Ancient Egypt, by Paul Ghalioungui, MD, MRCP, Senior Professor of Medicine, Faculty of Medicine, Ain Shams University.**

"We know of nine principal medical papyri. They are called after their original owners (Edwin Smith, Chester Beatty, Carlsberg), the site of their discovery (Kahoun, Ramesseum), the towns where they are kept (Leyden, London, Berlin) or their editor (Ebers).

The Kahoun Papyrus is the most ancient scroll and was discovered at Fayoum and was called by mistake the Kahoun Papyrus. It dates from 1950 B.C. And has on its back an account from the time of Amenemhat III (1840-1792 B.C.). Not only is this the oldest known papyrus, but the original from which it was copied seems also more antique than the originals of the other papyri.

It consists of three sections, one dealing with human medicine, the second with veterinary science, and the third with mathematics. It is written in hieratic handwriting like the other papyri, except the veterinary section which, possibly because of its greater antiquity, is written in hieroglyphic, a script usually reserved for theological writings.

The first two pages contain 17 gynaecological prescriptions and instructions without titles. No surgery is prescribed; substances recommended are beer, milk, oil, dates, herbs, incense and sometimes repulsive substances. Use is often made of fumigations, pastes, and vaginal applications.

The third page contains 17 prescriptions concerning the assessment of sterility and of pregnancy, and the ascertaining of the sex of unborn children. Many of the indications concerning pregnancy and childbirth refer to the state of the breasts, their firmness and to the color of the face and eyes."

Edwin Smith Papyrus: Dated to circa 1600 BCE, the Edwin Smith Papyrus is the only surviving copy of part of an Ancient Egyptian textbook on trauma surgery. The papyrus takes its name from the Egyptian archaeologist Edwin Smith, who purchased it in the 1860s

J.H. Breasted - **The Edwin Smith Surgical Papyrus (University of Chicago Press: University of Chicago, 1930)**

The most detailed and sophisticated of the extant medical papyri, it is also the world's oldest surgical text. Written in the hieratic script of the ancient Egyptian language, it is thought to be based on material from a thousand years earlier.

Robert H. Wilkins, (March 1964). "Neurosurgical Classic-XVII (Edwin Smith Surgical Papyrus)". Journal of Neurosurgery. 21 (3): 240–244. doi:10.3171/jns.1964.21.3.0240. translation of 13 cases from Breasted, James Henry (1930) pertaining to injuries of the skull and spinal cord, with commentary.

The document consists of 22 pages (17 pages on the recto, and 5 pages on the verso). 48 cases of trauma are examined, each with a description of the physical examination, diagnosis, treatment, and prognosis.

Austin Marry, (January 21, 2004). "Ancient Egyptian Medical Papyri". Ancient Egypt Fan. Eircom Limited.

48. Charles Richard Drew "Father of the Blood Bank" Renowned surgeon and pioneer in the preservation of life-saving blood plasma. "Dr. Charles Richard Drew broke barriers in a racially divided America to become one of the most important scientists of the 20th century. His pioneering research and systematic developments in the use and preservation of blood plasma during World War II not only saved thousands of lives, but innovated the nation's blood banking process and standardized procedures for long-term blood preservation and storage techniques adapted by the American Red Cross."
Full Biography available at:
www.acs.org/content/acs/en/education/whatischemistry/african-americans-in-sciences/charles-richard-drew.html

49. "Inventor Otis Boykin was born on August 29, 1920, in Dallas, Texas. After graduating from high school, he attended Fisk College in Nashville, Tennessee, graduating in 1941. Boykin, who took a special interest in working with resistors, began researching and inventing on his own. He sought and received a patent for a wire precision resistor on June 16, 1959.

This resistor would later be used in radios and televisions. Two years later, he created a breakthrough device that could withstand extreme changes in temperature and pressure. The device, which was cheaper and more reliable than others on the market, came in great demand by the United States military for guided missiles and IBM for computers.

In 1964, Boykin moved to Paris, creating electronic innovations for a new market of customers. His most famous invention was a control unit for the pacemaker. Ironically, Boykin died in Chicago in 1982 as a result of heart failure. Upon his death, he had 26 patents to his name."

'Otis Boykin' Biography.com, Biography.com Editors, Website Name, The Biography.com website, **www.biography.com/people/otis-boykin-538792**

50. "Onesimus was an enslaved man from Africa whose knowledge of smallpox inoculation was instrumental in the tradition being taken up in the United States. He was purchased as a slave for Cotton Mather, a Puritan church minister in Boston, by Mather's congregation in 1706. For his keen interests in science and medicine Mather had been elected as an honorary member of London's Royal Society in 1713. In a letter to the society sent in 1716, he records how Onesimus revealed to him a method of smallpox inoculation that he had undergone while still in Africa - he had the scar on his arm to confirm it. In 1721 Mather would use this knowledge to promote - against sometimes violent opposition - mass inoculation against smallpox when an epidemic of the disease struck Boston.

Because of his role in this act of knowledge transfer, Onesimus has a significant place in the history of smallpox inoculation. For an enslaved man, such a profile is unusual. The lives and voices of the vast majority of enslaved men, women and children are effectively lost to history - such was the inhumane nature of slavery. Alas, very little is known of Onesimus's life. He remains a fleeting figure in the historical record.

Mather may have acted on Onesimus's experience and knowledge of smallpox, but Onesimus remained a slave in the household and one that Mather eventually turned against. After failing to convert him to Christianity and considering him to be increasingly rebellious, Mather signed a conditional document in 1721 that allowed Onesimus to purchase his freedom - Onesimus having earlier given money toward the purchase of another black youth, Obadiah, to take his place. He also continued to do chores for the Mather family when required." – Via **www.sciencemuseum.org.uk/broughttolife/people/onesimus**

M Best, D Neuhauser, and L Slavin, '"Cotton Mather, you dog, dam you! I'll inoculate you with this; with a pox to you": smallpox inoculation, Boston, 1721' Quality and Safety in Healthcare, 13/1 (2004) pp 82-83

T H Brown, 'The African connection: Cotton Mather and the Boston smallpox epidemic of 1721-1722', Journal of the American Medical Association, 260 (1988) pp 2247-2249

K Silverman, The Life and Times of Cotton Mather (New York: Harper & Row, 1984)

Also reported by Boston Globe: "How an African slave helped Boston fight smallpox." - By Ted Widmer  October 17, 2014. - www.bostonglobe.com/ideas/2014/10/17/how-african-slave-helped-boston-fight-smallpox/XFhsMMvTGCeV62YP0XhhZI/story.html

## Politics

51. Bernard Alexander Montgomery Grant (17 February 1944 – 8 April 2000) was a British Labour Party politician who was the Member of Parliament for Tottenham from 1987 to his death in 2000.

https://en.wikipedia.org/wiki/Bernie_Grant

For Bernie Grant's full biography and ranking see:
www.100greatblackbritons.com/bios/bernie_grant.html

52. Ellen Johnson Sirleaf (born 29 October 1938) is a Liberian politician who serves as the 24th and current President of Liberia since 2006. Sirleaf is the first elected female head of state in Africa. She won the 2005 presidential election and took office on 16 January 2006, and she was re-elected in 2011...

For Ellen Johnson Sirleaf's full biography see:
www.forbes.com/profile/ellen-johnson-sirleaf/

Ellen Johnson Sirleaf - Facts". Nobelprize.org. Nobel Media AB 2014.
http://www.nobelprize.org/nobel_prizes/peace/laureates/2011/johnson_sirleaf-facts.html

53. Mozambique's first independent president Samora Moises Matchel: Editors of Encyclopædia Britannica
www.britannica.com/biography/Samora-Machel.

"the Mbuzini crash site was inaugurated on January 19, 1999, by Nelson Mandela and his wife Graça, and by President Joaquim Chissano of Mozambique. Now the monument is made professional and the memorial service is held on October 19 each year. Designed by Mozambican architect José Forjaz, at a cost to the South African government of 1.5 million Rand (US$300,000), the monument comprises 35 steel tubes symbolising the number of lives lost in the air crash. At least eight foreigners were killed there, including the four Soviet crew members, Machel's two Cuban doctors and the Zambian and Zairean ambassadors to Mozambique."

Monument for Machel plane crash site", Panafrican News Agency January 5, 1999: **https://en.wikipedia.org/wiki/Samora_Machel#Memorial**

54. "Olaudah Equiano (c. 1745 – 31 March 1797), known in his lifetime as Gustavus Vassa was a prominent African in London, a freed slave who supported the British movement to end the slave trade. His autobiography, published in 1789, helped in the creation of the Slave Trade Act 1807 which ended the African trade for Britain and its colonies."

**https://en.wikipedia.org/wiki/Olaudah_Equiano**

Robert King set Equiano to work on his shipping routes and in his stores. In 1765, when Equiano was about 20 years old, King promised that for his purchase price of 40 pounds (worth £6000 in the present day), the slave could buy his freedom.

**James Walvin, (2000). An African's Life: The Life and Times of Olaudah Equiano, 1745–1797. Continuum International Publishing Group. p. 71.**

By about 1767, Equiano had gained his freedom and went to England. He continued to work at sea, travelling sometimes as a deckhand based in England. In 1773 on the British Royal Navy Ship Racehorse, he travelled to the Arctic in an expedition to find a northern route to India.
He published his autobiography, The Interesting Narrative of the Life of Olaudah Equiano (1789), which depicted the horrors of slavery. It went through nine editions and aided passage of the British Slave Trade Act of 1807, which abolished the African slave trade. Since 1967, his memoir has been regarded as the "true beginning of modern African literature".

Olaudah Equiano, (1999). The Life of Olaudah Equiano, or, Gustavus Vassa, the African. Mineola, N.Y.: Dover Publications.

O. S. Ogede, "'The Igbo Roots of Olaudah Equiano' by Catherine Acholonu", Africa: Journal of the International African Institute, Vol. 61, No. 1, 1991, at JSTOR

For Olaudah Equiano's full biography see:
http://abolition.e2bn.org/people_25.html

55. For Diane Abbott's full biography see:
www.dianeabbott.org.uk/about.aspx;

100 Great Britons Ranking: www.100greatblackbritons.com/results.htm

For Paul Boatang's full biography see:
www.100greatblackbritons.com/bios/paul_boateng.html

For Bernie Grant's full biography see:
www.100greatblackbritons.com/bios/bernie_grant.html

## Rulers & Leaders

56. **Philippa of Hainault, 24 June 1314 – 15 August 1369 was Queen of England as the wife of King Edward III.**
**Strickland, Agnes, Lives of the queens of England from the Norman conquest, Vol.2, (George Barrie and Sons, 1902), 222**

Although visual evidence would suggest Phillipa was Caucasian, Bishop Stapledon of Exeter's written report upon meeting Phillipa reads as so: "The lady whom we saw has not uncomely hair, betwixt blue-black and brown. Her head is clean-shaped; her forehead high and broad, and standing somewhat forward. Her face narrows between the eyes, and the lower part of her face is still more narrow and slender than her forehead. Her eyes are blackish-brown and deep. **Her nose is fairly smooth and even, save that it is somewhat broad at the tip and also flattened, and yet it is no snub-nose. Her nostrils are also broad, her mouth fairly wide. Her lips somewhat full, and especially the lower lip.** Her teeth which have fallen and grown again are white enough, but the rest are not so white.

The lower teeth project a little beyond the upper; yet this is but little seen. Her ears and chin are comely enough. Her neck, shoulders, and all her body are well set and unmaimed; and nought is amiss so far as a man may see. **Moreover, she is brown of skin all over, and much like her father; and in all things she is pleasant enough**, as it seems to us. And the damsel will be of the age of nine years on St. John's day next to come, as her mother saith. She is neither too tall nor too short for such an age; she is of fair carriage, and well taught in all that becometh her rank, and highly esteemed and well beloved of her father and mother and of all her meinie, in so far as we could inquire and learn the truth."

The original document is written in Norman French. This is the translation derived from **The Register of Walter de Stapledon, Bishop of Exeter, 1307–1326, ed. F. C. Hingeston-Randolph (London, 1892), p.169. It is used in several books of the 1950s-60s, including G. G. Coulton, Medieval Panorama: The English Scene from Conquest to Reformation, Meridian Books, New York, 1955, p.644.; W. O. Hassal, How They Lived: An Anthology of Original Accounts Written before 1485, Blackwell, Oxford, 1962, p.95. However, Michael Prestwich's 2005 summary translates the description of the hair as "between blonde and brown" (the original is "entre bloy et brun"); Plantagenet England, 1225-1360 Clarendon, Oxford, 2005, p.215.**

Queen Phillipa's Regency see: **Strickland, Agnes. Lives of the Queens of England: From the Norman Conquest**
For Philippa of Hainault's full biography and ranking see:
**www.100greatblackbritons.com/bios/queen_phillipa.html**

57. Taytu Betul (c.1851–1918), wife of Menelik (King of Shoa and later Negus Negast or King of Kings), was a formidable queen and empress of Ethiopia.

She used her exceptional intelligence to strengthen and extend her power through an adroit blend of patronage, political marriages and leadership craft.
Determined to resist imperialist designs on her country, she increasingly opposed any negotiations that would result in the loss of Ethiopian territory. When diplomacy gave way to war, she rode out at the head of her own army, at her husband's side.

It was she who devised the plan which led to the Ethiopian victory at Makalle, and her presence was crucial in the Ethiopian victory at Adwa in 1896, the most significant victory of any African army during the climax of European colonialism.

She founded Addis Ababa, which remains Ethiopia's capital city today, and the final decades of her reign witnessed a period of modernization, which gradually opened Ethiopia up to trade and greater technical expertise.

She also provided the Ethiopian Orthodox Christian community in Jerusalem with dignified housing, and financed the construction of the dome of the impressive church Debre Genet. As her husband fell ill, she began to concentrate more and more power in her own hands. This eventually provoked public agitation against her, and forced her into retirement.

**http://en.unesco.org/womeninafrica/taytu-betul/biography**

For Taytu Betul's full biography see:
**www.encyclopedia.com/women/encyclopedias-almanacs-transcripts-and-maps/taytu-c-1850-1918**

58. Queen Charlotte, wife of the English King George III (1738-1820), was directly descended from Margarita de Castro y Sousa, a black branch of the Portuguese Royal House. The riddle of Queen Charlotte's African ancestry was solved as a result of an earlier investigation into the black magi featured in 15th century Flemish paintings. Two art historians had suggested that the black magi must have been portraits of actual contemporary people (since the artist, without seeing them, would not have been aware of the subtleties in colouring and facial bone structure of quadroons or octoroons which these figures invariably represented) Enough evidence was accumulated to propose that the models for the black magi were, in all probability, members of the Portuguese de Sousa family. (Several de Sousas had in fact travelled to the Netherlands when their cousin, the Princess Isabella went there to marry the Grand Duke, Philip the Good of Burgundy in the year 1429.)

Six different lines can be traced from English Queen Charlotte back to Margarita de Castro y Sousa, in a gene pool which because of royal inbreeding was already minuscule, thus explaining the Queen's unmistakable African appearance.

**www.pbs.org/wgbh/pages/frontline/shows/secret/famous/royalfamily.html**

"Her provision of funding to the General Lying-in Hospital in London prevented its closure; today it is named Queen Charlotte's and Chelsea Hospital, and is an acknowledged centre of excellence amongst maternity hospitals. A large copy of the Allan Ramsay portrait of Queen Charlotte hangs in the main lobby of the hospital."

**https://en.wikipedia.org/wiki/Charlotte_of_Mecklenburg-Strelitz**

59. "Queen Nanny or Nanny (c. 1686 – c. 1755), Jamaican National Hero, was a well-known, 18th-century leader of the Jamaican Maroons. Much of what is known about her comes from oral history, as little textual evidence exists. She was born into the Asante people in what is today Ghana, and escaped from slavery after being transported to Jamaica.
Wikipedia – **https://en.wikipedia.org/wiki/Nanny_of_the_Maroons**
Via - Government of Jamaica, national heroes listing
11 Facts about Queen Nany Via: **https://jamaicanechoes.com/11-facts-about-queen-nanny/**

60. Thomas Isidore Noël Sankara, 21 December 1949 – 15 October 1987) was a Burkinabé military captain, Marxist revolutionary, pan-Africanist and President of Burkina Faso from 1983-87.

Sankara seized power in a popularly-supported coup in 1983, aged just thirty-three, with the goal of eliminating corruption and the dominance of the former French colonial power.[1][5] He immediately launched one of the most ambitious programmes for social and economic change ever attempted on the African continent.[5] To symbolise this new autonomy and rebirth, he renamed the country from the French colonial Upper Volta to Burkina Faso ("Land of Upright Man").[5] His foreign policies were centered on anti-imperialism, with his government eschewing all foreign aid, pushing for odious debt reduction, nationalising all land and mineral wealth and averting the power and influence of the International Monetary Fund (IMF) and World Bank. His domestic policies were focused on preventing famine with agrarian self-sufficiency and land reform, prioritising education with a nationwide literacy campaign and promoting public health by vaccinating 2,500,000 children against meningitis, yellow fever and measles.

Other components of his national agenda included planting over 10,000,000 trees to halt the growing desertification of the Sahel, doubling wheat production by redistributing land from feudal landlords to peasants, suspending rural poll taxes and domestic rents and establishing an ambitious road and railway construction programme to "tie the nation together". On the localised level, Sankara also called on every village to build a medical dispensary, and had over 350 communities build schools with their own labour. Moreover, his commitment to women's rights led him to outlaw female genital mutilation, forced marriages and polygamy, while appointing women to high governmental positions and encouraging them to work outside the home and stay in school, even if pregnant.

Burkina Faso Salutes "Africa's Che" Thomas Sankara by Mathieu Bonkoungou

**Thomas Sankara Speaks: the Burkina Faso Revolution: 1983–87, by Thomas Sankara, edited by Michel Prairie; Pathfinder, 2007, pg 11 Thomas Sankara: The Upright Man by California Newsreel Commemorating Thomas Sankara by Farid Omar, Group for Research and Initiative for the Liberation of Africa (GRILA), November 28, 2007**

For Thomas Sankara's full biography see:
**https://en.wikipedia.org/wiki/Thomas_Sankara#cite_note-4**
Facts about Thomas Sankara in Burkina Faso: **http://africa-facts.org/facts-about-thomas-sankara-in-burkina-faso/**

61. Kwame Nkrumah, (born Sept. 1909, Nkroful, Gold Coast [now Ghana]—died April 27, 1972, Bucharest, Rom.), Ghanaian nationalist leader who led the Gold Coast's drive for independence from Britain and presided over its emergence as the new nation of Ghana. He headed the country from independence in 1957 until he was overthrown by a coup in 1966. For Kwame Nkrumah's full biography see:
**www.britannica.com/biography/Kwame-Nkrumah**

Ghana became independent on 6 March 1957. As the first of Britain's African colonies to gain majority-rule independence, the celebrations in

Accra were the focus of world attention; over 100 reporters and photographers covered the events. United States President Dwight D. Eisenhower sent congratulations and his vice president, Richard Nixon, to represent the U.S. at the events. The Soviet delegation urged Nkrumah to visit Moscow as soon as possible. Ralph Bunche, an African American, was there for the United Nations, while the Duchess of Kent represented Queen Elizabeth. Offers of assistance poured in from across the world. Even without them, the country seemed prosperous, with cocoa prices high and the potential of new resource development.

**David Rooney, (1988). Kwame Nkrumah: The Political Kingdom in the Third World. St. Martin's Press.**

**The Fifth Pan-African Congress was held in Manchester, United Kingdom, 15–21 October 1945. It followed the foundation of the Pan-African Federation in Manchester in 1944.**

**Hakim Adi, (2009), "George Padmore and the 1945 Manchester Pan-African Congress", in Baptiste, Fitzroy and Lewis, Rupert (eds), George Padmore: Pan-African Revolurionary. Kingston, Jamaica: Ian Randle**

Africans again fought in World War II. After this war, many felt that they now deserved independence. This Congress is widely considered to have been the most important. Organised by the influential Trinidadian pan-Africanist George Padmore and Ghanaian independence leader Kwame Nkrumah, it was attended by 90 delegates, 26 from Africa. They included many scholars, intellectuals and political activists who would later go on to become influential leaders in various African independence movements and the American civil rights movement, including the Kenyan independence leader Jomo Kenyatta, American activist and academic W. E. B. Du Bois, Malawi's Hastings Banda, Kwame Nkrumah of Ghana, prominent Jamaican barrister Dudley Thompson and Obafemi Awolowo and Jaja Wachuku from Nigeria. It also led partially to the creation of the Pan-African Federation, founded in 1946 by Nkrumah and Kenyatta.

Pan-Africanism is aimed at the economic, intellectual and political cooperation of the African countries. It demands that the riches of the continent be used for the enlistment of its people. It calls for the financial and economic unification of markets and a new political landscape for the continent. Even though Pan-Africanism as a movement began in 1776, it was the fifth Pan-African congress that advanced Pan-Africanism and applied it to decolonize the African continent.

**Motsoko Pheko (15 November 1999). "Road to Pan-Africanism"**

62. Pliny writes that the "Queen of the Ethiopians" bore the title Candace, and indicates that the Ethiopians had conquered ancient Syria and the Mediterranean.

**Sharon Turner, (1834). The Sacred History of the World, as Displayed in the Creation and Subsequent Events to the Deluge: Attempted to be Philosophically Considered, in a Series of Letters to a Son, Volume 2. Longman. pp. 480–482.**

In 25 BC the Kandake Amanirenas, as reported by Strabo, attacked the city of Syene, today's Aswan, in territory of the Roman Empire; Emperor Augustus destroyed the city of Napata in retaliation.

**Nubian Queens in the Nile Valley and Afro-Asiatic Cultural History Carolyn Fluehr-Lobban, Professor of Anthropology, Museum of Fine Arts, Boston U.S.A, August 20–26, 1998**

**E. A. Wallis Budge (2003), Cook's Handbook for Egypt and the Sudan, Part 2 (reprinted ed.), Kessinger Publishing, p. 737**

Kentake Amanirenas of Kush (flourished c.24 BC) Defender of the Sudanese Kingdom of Kush against Roman aggression

**Robin Walker – When We Ruled. www.whenweruled.com/?p=67**

63. Yanga, Gaspar (c. 1545- ?), Known as the Primer Libertador de America or "first liberator of the Americas," Gaspar Yanga led one of colonial Mexico's first successful slave uprisings and would go on to establish one of the Americas earliest free black settlements.

Rumored to be of royal lineage from West Africa, Yanga was an enslaved worker in the sugarcane plantations of Veracruz, Mexico. In 1570 he, along with a group of followers, escaped, fled to the mountainous regions near Córdoba, and established a settlement of former slaves or palenque. They remained there virtually unmolested by Spanish authorities for nearly 40 years. Taking the role of spiritual and military leader, he structured the agricultural community in an ordered capacity, allowing its growth and occupation of various locations.

During that time, Yanga and his band, also known as cimarrónes, were implicated in the disruption and looting of trade goods along the Camino Real (Royal Road) between Veracruz and Mexico City. They were also held responsible for attacking nearby haciendas and kidnapping indigenous women. Perceived as dangerous to the colonial system of slavery through their daring actions against royal commerce and authority, New Spain's viceroy called for the annihilation of Yanga's palenque. Destroying the community and its leader would send a message to other would-be rebellious slaves that Spain's authority over them was absolute.

In 1609, Spanish authorities sent a well-armed militia to defeat Yanga and his palenque but were defeated. Yanga's surprise victory over the Spanish heightened the confidence of his warriors and the frustration in Mexico City.

After defeating other Spanish forces sent again the palenque, Yanga offered to make peace but with eleven conditions, the most important being recognition of the freedom of all of the palenque's residents prior to 1608, acknowledgment of the settlement as a legal entity which Yanga and his descendants would govern, and the prohibition of any Spanish in the community. Yanga, in turn, promised to serve and pay tribute to the Spanish crown. After years of negotiations, in 1618, the town of San Lorenzo de Los Negros was officially recognized by Spanish authorities as a free black settlement. It would later be referred to as Yanga, named after its founder.

**http://www.blackpast.org/gah/yanga-gaspar-c-1545**

64. J. A. Rodgers, the inspiration for this title in his works 'Sex and Race' p. 198 says "We see one of the Black people – the Moors of the Romans- in the person of a King of Alban of the tenth century. History knows him as Dubh, and as Niger... We know as a historical fact that a Niger Vel Dubh has lived and reigned over certain black divisions of our islands – and probably white divisions also."

Rodgers cited: **Ancient and Modern Britons, Vol I, pp. 12,121,131, Vol.II pp. 17, 20, 87, 102, 107, 112, 113, 127, 189-9, 297, 322, 328-329, 360, 392.**

https://archive.org/stream/sexAndRacevol.1/SexAndRaceVol.1#page/n1 11/mode/2up/search/kenneth

65. "Patrice Lumumba was the first prime minister of the Democratic Republic of Congo, calling for national unity and overall African independence.

Born on July 2, 1925, in Onalua, Belgian Congo (now the Democratic Republic of the Congo), Patrice Lumumba was a writer and civic organizer before co-founding the Congolese National Movement. He became the first prime minister of the Democratic Republic of Congo with the country's independence; yet massive unrest followed with other leaders' uprisings, along with U.S. and Belgian involvement. Lumumba was killed on January 17, 1961."

For Patrice Lumumba's full biography see:
**www.britannica.com/biography/Patrice-Lumumba**

"Lumumba, who was not scheduled to speak, delivered an impromptu speech that reminded the audience that the independence of the Congo was not granted magnanimously by Belgium

**"Independence Day Speech". Africa Within**
www.marxists.org/subject/africa/lumumba/1960/06/independence.htm
"For this independence of the Congo, even as it is celebrated today with Belgium, a friendly country with whom we deal as equal to equal, no Congolese worthy of the name will ever be able to forget that it was by fighting that it has been won, a day-to-day fight, an ardent and idealistic fight, a fight in which we were spared neither privation nor suffering, and for which we gave our strength and our blood. We are proud of this struggle, of tears, of fire, and of blood, to the depths of our being, for it was a noble and just struggle, and indispensable to put an end to the humiliating slavery which was imposed upon us by force."

**Africa 1960-1970: Chronicle and Analysis, Godfrey Mwakikagile, New Africa Press, 2009, page 20.**

Most European journalists were shocked by the stridency of Lumumba's speech. The Belgians thereafter regarded him as an implacable political threat.

**David N. Gibbs, (1 November 1991). The Political Economy of Third World Intervention: Mines, Money, and U.S. Policy in the Congo Crisis. American Politics and Political Economy. University of Chicago Press.**

66. "Just before dawn on May 13, 1862, Robert Smalls and a crew composed of fellow slaves, in the absence of the white captain and his two mates, slipped a cotton steamer off the dock, picked up family members at a rendezvous point, then slowly navigated their way through the harbor. Smalls, doubling as the captain, even donning the captain's wide-brimmed straw hat to help to hide his face, responded with the proper coded signals at two Confederate checkpoints, including at Fort Sumter itself, and other defense positions. Cleared, Smalls sailed into the open seas. Once outside of Confederate waters, he had his crew raise a white flag and surrendered his ship to the blockading Union fleet.

    In fewer than four hours, Robert Smalls had done something unimaginable: In the midst of the Civil War, this black male slave had commandeered a heavily armed Confederate ship and delivered its 17 black passengers (nine men, five women and three children) from slavery to freedom."

    Which Slave Sailed Himself to Freedom? by Henry Louis Gates, Jr.
    **www.pbs.org/wnet/african-americans-many-rivers-to-cross/history/which-slave-sailed-himself-to-freedom/**
    **For Robert Smalls full biography see** www.biography.com/people/robert-smalls-9486288

### Sports

67. Considered one of the greatest boxers of all time, Sugar Ray Robinson held the world welterweight title from 1946 to 1951, and by 1958, he had become the first boxer to win a divisional world championship five times.

    Sugar Ray Robinson was born Walker Smith Jr. on May 3, 1921.
    **www.biography.com/people/sugar-ray-robinson-9461060**

Robinson was 85–0 as an amateur with 69 of those victories coming by way of knockout, 40 in the first round. He turned professional in 1940 at the age of 19 and by 1951 had a professional record of 128–1–2 with 84 knockouts. From 1943 to 1951 Robinson went on a 91-fight unbeaten streak, the third longest in professional boxing history.

http://boxrec.com/en/boxer/9625
https://web.archive.org/web/20150406100401/http://www.africanring
magazine.com/Aug-Sept-2011/unbeaten-streak.html

Robinson began his career with an astonishing 40 straight victories and was called the "uncrowned champion" by boxing fans on account that the mob, who Robinson refused to play nice with, denied him the chance to fight for the world welterweight title until after the war. When Robinson finally did get his shot at the belt in 1946, he took home the crown with a unanimous 15-round decision over Tommy Bell; Robinson would hold the welterweight title until 1951. Six years later, Robinson captured the middleweight title for the first time by defeating Jake LaMotta. By 1958, he had become the first boxer to win a divisional world championship five times.

Robinson finally retired from the sport for good in 1965. Two years later, he was inducted into the International Boxing Hall of Fame.
In 1984 The Ring magazine placed Robinson No. 1 in its book "The 100 Greatest Boxers of All Time."

www.biography.com/people/sugar-ray-robinson-9461060

68. Coached at Texas Southern by former Olympic champion, [Bobby Morrow], Jim Hines made track history at the 1968 AAU when he became the first man to better 10 seconds for 100m. He clocked a windy 9.8 that day in the heats, but had a legal 9.9 in the semis before losing the final to Charlie Greene, both runners recording a windy 10.0. In Mexico, Hines won the gold medal in 9.95 which was a world record for automatic timing. In the relay Hines took the baton in third place, but ran an outstanding anchor leg to give the U.S. a victory and another world record. After the 1968 Olympic season, Hines turned professional and had a brief career in pro football with the Miami Dolphins.

www.sports-reference.com/olympics/athletes/hi/jim-hines-1.html

During the 1968 Summer Olympics held in Mexico City, the African-American sprinter Jim Hines earned the title of 'fastest man on the planet' when he broke the long-standing 10-second barrier in the 100 m event. With a time of 9.95 sec, Hines stormed to Olympic gold and established a 100 m world record that remained unbeaten for 15 years. Astonishingly, he would go on to better his time at the very same Olympics, running the anchor leg of the 4 x 100 m relay event in just 8.2 sec. Jim Hines achieved a time of 9.9 sec in his semi-final at the AAU championships held in Sacramento on 20 June 1968, but this was manually.

www.guinnessworldrecords.com/world-records/first-person-to-run-100-m-in-less-than-10-seconds-(automatic-timing)

69. Usain Bolt enhanced his already legendary Olympic status with an unprecedented third consecutive 100m, 200m and 4x100m triple at Rio 2016, a feat that may well never be repeated. The holder of the world records at all three distances and an 11-time world champion, the Jamaican star bid farewell to the Olympic stage by celebrating his 30th birthday on the day of the Closing Ceremony of the Rio Games.

Between 16 August 2008 and 19 August 2016, Usain Bolt won 20 Olympic and world championship gold medals in the 21 events he entered, a staggering tally that makes him the greatest sprinter of all time. After winning his third consecutive Olympic 100m title in Rio, the Jamaican great was moved to comment: "Somebody said I can become immortal. Two more medals to go and I can sign off. Immortal."

Then, after completing his "triple-double" with a third straight Olympic 200m triumph, he announced that he wanted to be up there with the very best of them all: "I am trying to be one of the greatest, among Ali and Pele." And after crossing the line first in the 4x100m final and joining Finland's Paavo Nurmi and the USA's Carl Lewis as a nine-time Olympic gold medallist, an elated Bolt commented: "There you go, I'm the greatest. I'm just happy to have done what I came here to do. I'm proud of myself. The pressure is real, but I look at it as an accomplishment."

A brilliant junior athlete, Bolt made his Olympic debut as a 17-year-old at Athens 2004, where, hampered by a torn hamstring, he went out in the opening round of the 200m. Yet by the time he returned to the Games at Beijing four years later, the tall Jamaican sprinter was a firm favourite to claim an Olympic sprint double, having set a new 100m world record of 9.72 seconds in late May in New York, followed by the fastest 200m of the year, 19.67, a few weeks later in the Greek capital.

Taking to the track at the Bird's Nest in his distinctive gold spikes, Bolt duly etched his name in track and field history, trimming his world record to 9.69 and winning the 100m at a canter, so much so that he was celebrating victory with arms outstretched 20 metres from the line. Another gold and another world record followed in the 200m, with the Jamaican clocking 19.30 to eclipse Michael Johnson's time at Atlanta 1996. A third gold and a third world record followed in the 4x100m relay, Bolt running a lightning-fast final bend as he, Nesta Carter, Michael Frater and Asafa Powell clocked 37.10 between them.

"I want to share it with my team," said Bolt after completing his hat-trick. "It's down to them that I beat the world record today. When you beat the relay world record, you feel four times happier." His unprecedented achievement of setting three world records in winning three sprint golds made him the star of Beijing 2008 along with US swimmer Michael Phelps, and earned him an ecstatic reception on his return to Jamaica in early September.

Bolt consolidated his status as a global superstar at the IAAF World Championships in Berlin the following year, trimming 0.11 seconds off his 100m world record, taking it down to 9.58, and setting a new 200m world record of 19.19. Both times are yet to be beaten.

The only major title that eluded by Bolt after Beijing 2008 was the 100m at the 2011 Worlds in Daegu, where he was disqualified for a false start in the final. Determined to atone for that setback, he arrived at London 2012 with his sights firmly set on more gold. Savouring the atmosphere in the British capital, Bolt said: "What I liked about London was definitely the crowd. For me, it was the energy, and surprisingly the stadium was always full, no matter what time of day. I came out for the heats of the 100m, which was early, and it was ram-packed of people. It was a great reception. It was a wonderful experience."

Bolt drew on that energy to retain the 100m, 200m and 4x100m titles, the Jamaican star linking up with Frater, Carter and Yohan Blake in the last of those three events to run 36.84, yet another world record. Reflecting on his unprecedented second "triple triple", he said: "There was a little bit more pressure, but it didn't bother me as much. But there was a different expectation from me. I went out there just to show the world that I could do it again. That was my focus and I got it done, so it was good. It was a long season but I accomplished what I came to London to do. I'm very proud of myself."

Further world championship triples came at Moscow in 2013 and Beijing in 2015, taking his collection of world titles to a staggering 11, more than any other athlete. In collecting his massive array of golds, the Jamaican made his signature "Shh" gesture and "Lightning Bolt" celebration pose a familiar sight at arenas all over the world.

When it came to confirming his supremacy in his three events at Rio 2016, the Jamaican superstar had to dig deeper than ever, coming from behind in the last 50 metres to win the 100m in a time of 9.81, and then grimacing as he crossed the line in the 200m in 19.78, his slowest time in a major championship. "I don't know about the 200m in the future," he said afterwards. "Next year at the World Championships it will likely just be the 100m, even though my coach keeps trying to convince me otherwise. But personally for me, I think this is the last time I will run the 200m. I wasn't happy with the time and my body did not respond down the straight. But I'm getting older, so I am pleased to get the gold medal."

After winning the 4x100m title in Brazil with Asafa Powell, Nickel Ashmeade and Blake to make it nine Olympic golds out of nine, Bolt confirmed that he had made his last appearance at the Games and that the 2017 World Championships in London would be his swansong as an athlete. Explaining the recipe for his success, he said: "It's hard work, sweat and sacrifice. I've sacrificed so much throughout the season, throughout the years. I've been through so much. I knew this moment would come. I've got mixed feelings about it. I don't have the words to describe my three trebles. I'm going to miss this sport and I'm going to miss the Games because it's the biggest event possible for any athlete. But I've proven that I'm the greatest in this sport and, for me, it's mission accomplished."

Taken from Usain Bolts Segment on the official Olympic Website: **www.olympic.org/usain-bolt**

70. Serena Williams just picked up her 23rd Grand Slam title, defeating her "toughest opponent" — her big sister Venus. The 6-4, 6-4 Australian Open win catapulted her in front of 22-Grand Slam winner Steffi Graf, and gave Williams the title for most Grand Slams in the Open era of anyone, male or female.

The victory, following a year in which Serena won one Grand Slam and lost her No. 1 world ranking to Germany's Angelique Kerber, recaptures her world ranking.

Both Serena and Venus Williams entered the professional tennis circuit in the 1990s. Their tenure has been long, their dominance persistent, and their absences — for injuries and illnesses — brief. They've come a long way from training on the public courts in Compton, California, where as kids, they would duck when gunshots rang out.

**www.pbs.org/newshour/rundown/serena-williams-breaks-record-23rd-grand-slam/**

For a list of Serena Williams Career Achievements see:
**https://en.wikipedia.org/wiki/List_of_career_achievements_by_Serena_Williams**

Williams has been ranked world No. 1 by the Women's Tennis Association on three occasions, for a total of 11 weeks. She first became the world No. 1 on February 25, 2002, the first African American woman to do so in the Open Era. Her seven Grand Slam singles titles puts her in a tie for 12th on the all-time list, and a tie for 8th on the Open Era list, more than any other active female player except her sister Serena. In total, she has reached sixteen Grand Slam finals, the most recent being the finals at Wimbledon in 2017. She has also won 14 Grand Slam Women's doubles titles, all with her sister Serena, and the pair are unbeaten in Grand Slam doubles finals; Venus also has two Mixed doubles titles. Her five Wimbledon singles titles ties her with two other women for eighth place on the all-time list, but gives her sole possession of No. 4 on the Open Era List, only trailing Navratilova's 9 titles and Serena's and Graf's 7 titles. From the 2000 Wimbledon Championships to the 2001 US Open, Williams won four of the six Grand Slam singles tournaments held. At the 2017 Wimbledon Championships, Williams extended her record as the all-time leader, male or female, in Grand Slams played, with 75. Williams' run to the 2017

Wimbledon singles final also broke the record for time elapsed between first and most recent grand slam singles finals appearances.

https://en.wikipedia.org/wiki/Venus_Williams

71. Ibtihaj Muhammad, the American fencer who had just lost to Cecilia Berder, of France, in the round of 16 at the women's individual saber event in Rio, coyly replied with a smile. Her dream of winning an individual medal at her first Olympics had just ended, but Muhammad was unwilling to cede her moment.

    The first American athlete to compete in the Olympics wearing a hijab, Muhammad has a platform far more prominent than that of most fencers, or even most Olympians. The other members of Team USA nearly voted her to carry the opening ceremonies flag — she trailed only Michael Phelps.

    What Muhammad hasn't failed to do, however, is embrace role as an ambassador for Muslim-American women. "I want to break cultural barriers," she says. "I feel like this moment, representing my country and the Muslim community, it's bigger than myself."

    Reported by Time: **http://time.com/4443648/rio-2016-olympics-ibtihaj-muhammad-hijab-history/**

72. "Simone Manuel breaks down in tears as she becomes the first black woman to win an Olympic swimming gold medal - but she SHARES it with Canadian after dramatic tie"

    Simone Manuel made history as first US black woman to medal in an individual Olympic swimming event. The 20-year-old won gold in the women's 100m freestyle race - setting a new Olympic record in process Manuel, who came joint first with Canada's Penny Oleksiak, gave USA first gold in the event since 1984
    Full Report Available At the Daily Mail:
    **http://www.dailymail.co.uk/news/article-3735602/Simone-Manuel-20-black-woman-win-individual-Olympic-swimming-gold-stunning-100m-freestyle-TIE-Canadian-rival.html#ixzz4saTjLO3B**

73. Former Brazilian international Edson Arantes do Nascimento or 'Pele' is arguably the greatest footballer of all time. He is the holder of many footballing records and even after so many decades some of his records still stand.

Pele is the all-time leading goalscorer for Brazil with 77 goals in 91 games and has 15 goals more than Ronaldo Nazario who scored 62 goals in 98 games. A few years back it looked like no player would be able to break that record, but considering the pace at which Neymar is racking up goals for the Selecao, the Barcelona man could break the record in a few years. After all, he is just 24 and has already scored 46 international goals.

Pele is the only footballer ever to win the World Cup on three occasions. Brazil have won the FIFA World Cup five times and Pele was part of three of those teams. He won back to back titles in 1958 and 1962 before lifting his third and final one in 1970.

Pele is the only footballer ever to win the World Cup on three occasions. Brazil have won the FIFA World Cup five times and Pele was part of three of those teams. He won back to back titles in 1958 and 1962 before lifting his third and final one in 1970.

Pele has scored a record 92 hat-tricks in his career. This comprises of 21.5% of the goals he has scored in his career. He is also credited with six five-goal hauls and scored four in a game on 31 occasions.

Aged just 17 years and 244 days, Pele scored a hat-trick in the semi-final of the 1958 FIFA World Cup against France. This feat was five days after he became the youngster scorer in a world cup – a record he still holds.

When Pele played for the first time in a FIFA World Cup in 1958, he became the youngest player to play in a World Cup, but the record was broken later. However, his records for being the youngest scorer and the youngest hat-trick scorer in the tournament still stands.

In the final of the 1958 edition, Pele set one more record which stands true even today. During the final against host nation Sweden, Pele scored a brace of which the first one is considered as one of the greatest goals in the history of the FIFA World Cup.

His two goals in the final was when he was just 17 years and 249 days old. These goals also took his tally for the tournament to six, which put him joint second behind Just Fontaine.

www.sportskeeda.com/slideshow/football-5-pele-records-likely-stand-forever?imgid=81950

74. Francis Morgan Ayodélé "Daley" Thompson, CBE (born 30 July 1958), is an English former decathlete. He won the decathlon gold medal at the Olympic Games in 1980 and 1984, and broke the world record for the event four times.

    With four world records, two Olympic gold medals, three Commonwealth titles, and wins in the World and European Championships, Thompson is considered by many to be one of the greatest decathletes of all time. Robert Chalmers described him as "the greatest all-round athlete this country [United Kingdom] has ever produced."

    Thompson opened the 1980 Olympic season with a world decathlon record of 8,648 points at Götzis, Austria, in May, and followed this with a comfortable win at the Moscow Olympics. After a quiet 1981 season, he was in devastating form in 1982; back at Götzis in May, he raised the world record to 8,730 points and then in September, at the European Championships in Athens, he took the record up to 8,774 points. The following month in Brisbane, Thompson took his second Commonwealth title. In 1983, Daley won the inaugural World Championships and became the first decathlete to hold a continental title, in his case the European title, and the World and Olympic titles simultaneously. He also became by virtue of his World title, the first athlete in any athletics event to hold Olympic, World, continental and Commonwealth Games titles in a single event simultaneously.

    He spent much of the summer of 1984 in California preparing for the defence of his Olympic title, with Jürgen Hingsen, the West German who had succeeded Thompson as the world record holder, expected to be a major threat. Thompson took the lead in the first event and was never headed throughout the competition, although it seemed that, by easing off in the 1,500 metres he had missed tying the world record by just one point. When the photo-finish pictures were examined, however, it was found that Thompson should have been credited with one more point in the 110 metres hurdles so he had in fact, equalled Hingsen's record. Then when the new scoring tables were introduced, Thompson became the sole record holder once more with a recalculated score of 8,847 points – a world record that stood until 1992, when it was surpassed by the American athlete Dan O'Brien with a score of 8891. His two victories in the Olympic decathlon are a feat shared only with the Americans Bob Mathias and Ashton Eaton. Thompson's 1984 performance is still the UK record.

**https://en.wikipedia.org/wiki/Daley_Thompson**

75. Wilma Rudolph (1940–1994) was considered the fastest woman in the world in the '60s, and the first American woman to win three gold medals in track & field in the 1960 Olympics.

This was the first year that the Olympics were covered internationally on television, which helped Wilma become an international star. In the 1960 Rome Olympics, she was known as "The Tornado"; in France, "La Perle Noire" ("The Black Pearl"); to the Italians she was "La Gazzella Negra" ("The Black Gazelle").

Wilma had to overcome a childhood filled with challenges. She was born prematurely, but because of the racial segregation at the time, Wilma and her mother Blanche were turned away from the local hospital. The family's budget was very tight — Wilma was the 20th of her father's 22 children from two marriages. They could barely afford the one local black doctor, so Wilma was nursed to health by her mother and tight-knit family.

As a child, Wilma seemed to contract one illness after another. She went through bouts of measles, mumps, scarlet fever, chicken pox, and pneumonia. At age 4, she contracted infantile paralysis caused by the polio virus. Though she recovered from the virus, she had to wear a brace on her left leg and foot in order to walk.

Wilma had a loving family who cared deeply for each other. Her mother Blanche took her to a hospital 50 miles a way, twice a week, for two years until she was able to walk without the braces.

By the time she was 16 — just 4 years after fully recovering from her paralysis — Wilma earned a place on the US Olympic track and field team in 1956, where she earned a bronze medal.

In the 1960 Olympics, Wilma became an international star as "the fastest woman in history". She flew through the 100 meter, 200 meter, and 4 X 100 relay, winning three gold medals. She set world records in the 200 meter dash, winning it in 23.2 seconds, and in the relay, winning along with her teammates in 44.5 seconds.

After her incredible performance, Wilma returned home to Tennessee to find out the Governor was planning a welcome-home celebration. Wilma refused to attend her own celebration since the event would be segregated. Because of her protest, Wilma's parade and banquet were the very first integrated events in her hometown of Clarksville. She went on to participate in protests in the city until the segregation laws were struck down.

www.amazingwomeninhistory.com/wilma-rudolph-olympic-gold-medalist-civil-right-pioneer/

76. Charles Lewis Haley (born January 6, 1964) is a former American football linebacker and defensive end who played in the National Football League (NFL) for the San Francisco 49ers (1986–1991, 1998–1999) and the Dallas Cowboys (1992–1996).

A versatile defensive player, Haley began his career as a specialty outside linebacker, eventually progressing to pass-rusher and finally full-fledged defensive end. He is the first five-time Super Bowl champion, and is one of only two such players, the other being Tom Brady.

https://en.wikipedia.org/wiki/Charles_Haley

77. Simone Biles has won a total of 19 Olympic and world championship titles, making her the most decorated gymnast in the United States. She took this title from Shannon Miller.

Biles earned a gold in the all-around, vault and floor in the 2016 Olympics in Rio de Janeiro. She was also part of the gold medallist team that became known as the Final Five. She now holds the records for the most golds won in women's gymnastics in a single Olympics.

She has earned three world all-around championship titles; three world floor championships; two world balance beam championships. Her list of amazing accolades goes on. She was even named an all-around champion in the U.S. nationals four times.

In addition, Simone Biles bested Liukin and Miller in world championships success. And in her years as a senior, Biles proved that she was one of the most talented and dominant gymnasts the U.S. had ever seen.
The Best American Gymnasts Ever, by Amy Van Deusen Updated August 07, 2017:

**www.thoughtco.com/top-american-gymnasts-1714744**

## Warfare

78. King Houegbadja (who ruled from 1645 to 1685), the third King of Dahomey, is said to have originally started the group which would become the Amazons as a corps of elephant hunters called the gbeto.

Houegbadja's son King Agaja (ruling from 1708 to 1732) established a female bodyguard armed with muskets. European merchants recorded their presence. According to tradition, Agaja developed the bodyguard into a militia and successfully used them in Dahomey's defeat of the neighbouring kingdom of Savi in 1727. The group of female warriors was referred to as N'Nonmiton, meaning "Our Mothers" in the Fon language, by the male army of Dahomey.

From the time of King Ghezo (ruling from 1818 to 1858), Dahomey became increasingly militaristic. Ghezo placed great importance on the army, increasing its budget and formalizing its structure from ceremonial to a serious military. While European narratives refer to the women soldiers as "Amazons," they called themselves ahosi (king's wives) or N'Nonmiton (our mothers)
Dahomey Amazons: **https://en.wikipedia.org/wiki/Dahomey_Amazons**
Ghezo recruited both men and women soldiers from foreign captives, though women soldiers were also recruited from free Dahomian women, some enrolled as young as 8 years old.

The women soldiers were rigorously trained, given uniforms, and equipped with Danish guns (obtained via the slave trade). By the mid-19th century, they numbered between 1,000 and 6,000 women, about a third of the entire Dahomey army, according to reports written by visitors. The reports also noted variously that the women soldiers suffered several defeats, but that the women soldiers were consistently judged to be superior to the male soldiers in effectiveness and bravery.

**Robin Law, (1993). "The 'Amazons' of Dahomey". Paideuma. 39: 245–260**

79. With the beginning of World War II African Americans would get their chance to be in "the toughest outfit going," the previously all-white Marine Corps. The first recruits reported to Montford Point, a small section of land on Camp Lejeune, North Carolina on August 26, 1942. By October only 600 recruits had begun training although the call was for 1,000 for combat in the 51st and 52nd Composite Defense Battalions.

Initially the recruits were trained by white officers and non-commissioned officers (NCOs) but citing a desire to have blacks train blacks, the Marines quickly singled out several exceptional black recruits to serve as NCO drill instructors. In January 1943, Edgar R. Huff became the first black NCO as a private first class. In February Gilbert "Hashmark" Johnson, a 19-year veteran of the Army and Navy, became the first Drill Sergeant. By May 1943 all training at Montford Point was done by black sergeants and drill instructors (DIs), with Johnson as chief DI. Both Johnson and Huff would be renowned throughout the entire Marine Corps for their demanding training and exceptional leadership abilities.

The men of the 51st soon distinguished themselves as the finest artillery gunners in the Marine Corps, breaking almost every accuracy record in training. Unfortunately, discrimination towards African American fighting abilities still existed and when shipped to the Pacific, the 51st and 52nd were posted to outlying islands away from the primary action. The only Montfort Marines to see action, and record casualties, were the Ammunition and Depot Companies in Saipan, Guam, and Peleliu. Private Kenneth Tibbs was the first black Marine to lose his life on June 15, 1944. The Montford Point Marine training facility was abolished in 1949 after President Harry S. Truman issued Executive Order 9981 which desegregated the U.S. Armed Forces.

**Montford Point Marines (1942-1949):**
**www.blackpast.org/aah/montford-point-marines-1942-1945**

America's first black Marines decorated with congressional medals 70 years after graduating from segregated boot camp Montford Point: **www.dailymail.co.uk/news/article-2190761/Americas-African-American-Marines-Montford-Point-decorated-congressional-medals-70-years-later.html#ixzz4sgyqUczn**

80. While on board the latter in 1966 for the recovery of a nuclear weapon off Spain, Brashear was badly injured in an accident; as a result, surgeons amputated his left leg below the knee. He refused to submit to medical survey boards attempting to retire him as unfit for duty. After demonstrating that he could still dive and perform his other duties, he served in Harbor Clearance Unit 2, Naval Air Station Norfolk, Experimental Diving Unit, submarine tender Hunley (AS-31); USS Recovery (ARS-43), Naval Safety Center, and Shore Intermediate Maintenance Activity Norfolk.

    In 1970, he qualified as the first black master diver in the history of the U.S. Navy. Master Chief Brashear's memoir also includes material on his divorced in 1978 and his post-retirement employment and a candid description of his treatment in the Navy's alcohol rehabilitation program. April 1, 1979, he retired from the Navy as a master chief petty officer and master diver.

    Carl Brashear: Black First Navy: **www.aaregistry.org/historic_events/view/carl-brashear-black-first-navy**

    In April 1968, after a long struggle, Brashear was the first amputee diver to be (re)certified as a U.S. Navy diver. In 1970, he became the first African-American U.S. Navy Master Diver, and served nine more years beyond that, achieving the rating of Master Chief Boatswain's Mate in 1971

    **https://en.wikipedia.org/wiki/Carl_Brashear#Leg_amputation_and_recovery**

### Miscellaneous

81. Maurice Ashley (born March 6, 1966) is a Jamaican American chess grandmaster, author, commentator, app designer, puzzle inventor, and motivational speaker. In 1992, Ashley shared the United States Game/10 chess championship with Maxim Dlugy. Fédération Internationale des

94

Échecs or World Chess Federation (FIDE) awarded him the grandmaster title in 1999, making him the world's first Jamaican chess International Grandmaster.

**https://en.wikipedia.org/wiki/Maurice_Ashley**

For Maurice Ashley's full biography see: **www.mauriceashley.com**

82. Sir Trevor McDonald, OBE (born George McDonald; 16 August 1939) is a Trinidadian-British newsreader and journalist, best known for his career as a news presenter with ITN. McDonald was knighted in 1999 for his services to journalism.
**https://en.wikipedia.org/wiki/Trevor_McDonald#News_at_Ten**

For Trevor McDonalds, Black Britons ranking see:
**http://www.100greatblackbritons.com/results.htm**

For Trevor McDonalds ranking see:
**www.100greatblackbritons.com/bios/queen_phillipa.html**

For Trevor McDonalds, full biography see:
**www.biogs.com/broadcasters/mcdonald.html**

83. The Association for the Study of Classical African Civilizations (ASCAC) is an independent study group organization founded in 1984 by Drs. John Henrik Clark, Asa Grant Hilliard, Leonard Jeffries, Jacob H. Carruthers, Rkhty Amen, Yosef Ben-Jochannan, and Maulana Karenga that is devoted to the rescue, reconstruction, and restoration of African history and culture. It is an organization that provides the opportunity for "African peoples to educate other African peoples about their culture."

ASCAC was founded by scholars with ties to African-American communities in New York City, Chicago, Atlanta, and Los Angeles and derives its membership from African Americans across class and occupational locations. The organization has since expanded into an international organization, with membership regions representing the continental United States, as well as the Caribbean, Africa, and Europe. ASCAC has four commissions which advance this agenda: education, research, spiritual development, and creative production. Along with creating study groups throughout the world, ASCAC holds an annual conference, operates a youth enrichment program, and is editing a comprehensive history of Africa.

**https://en.wikipedia.org/wiki/Association_for_the_Study_of_Classical_African_Civilizations**

For more information about ongoing ASCAC projects, conferences and events visit their official website: **www.ascacfoundation.org/mission/**

84. In 1906, Gurley moved to Tulsa where he purchased 40 acres of land which was "only to be sold to colored". Black ownership was unheard of at that time. An educator and entrepreneur who made his wealth as a landowner, Gurley purchased 40 acres in Tulsa to be sold to "coloreds only."

Gurley's property lines were Pine Street to the north, the Frisco rail tracks to the south, Lansing Avenue to the east and Cincinnati Avenue to the west. This road was given the name Greenwood Avenue, named for the city in Mississippi. The area became very popular among African American migrants fleeing the oppression in Mississippi. They would find refuge in Gurley's building, as the racial persecution from the south was non-existent on Greenwood Avenue. In addition to his rooming house, Gurley built three two-story buildings and five residences and bought an 80-acre (320,000 m2) farm in Rogers County. Gurley also founded what is today Vernon AME Church.

Gurley's prominence, influence and wealth were short lived. In a matter of moments, he lost everything. During the race war, The Gurley Hotel at 112 N. Greenwood, the street's first commercial enterprise, valued at $55,000, was lost, and with it Brunswick Billiard Parlor and Dock Eastmand & Hughes Cafe. Gurley also owned a two-story building at 119 N. Greenwood. It housed Carter's Barbershop, Hardy Rooms, a pool hall, and cigar store. All were reduced to ruins. By his account and court records, he lost nearly $200,000 in the 1921 race war.

**www.blackwallstreet.org/owgurly**

Thirty-five city blocks went up in flames, 300 people died, and 800 were injured.

Since the blacks were outnumbered, they headed back to Greenwood. But the enraged whites were not far behind, looting and burning businesses and homes along the way.

Nine thousand people became homeless, Josie Pickens writes in Ebony. This "modern, majestic, sophisticated, and unapologetically black" community boasted of "banks, hotels, cafés, clothiers, movie theatres, and contemporary homes." Not to mention luxuries, such as "indoor plumbing and a remarkable school system that superiorly educated black children." Undoubtedly, less fortunate white neighbours resented their upper-class lifestyle. As a result of a jealous desire "to put progressive, high-achieving African-Americans in their place," a wave of domestic white terrorism caused black dispossession.

Gurley provided an opportunity for those migrating "from the harsh oppression of Mississippi." The average income of black families in the area exceeded "what minimum wage is today." As a result of segregation, a "dollar circulated 36 to 100 times" and remained in Greenwood "almost a year before leaving." Even more impressive, at that time, the "state of Oklahoma had only two airports," yet "six black families owned their own planes."

**https://daily.jstor.org/the-devastation-of-black-wall-street/**

First Aerial Bombardment in the US: The first of these incidents occurred in Tulsa, Oklahoma, in 1921. In May of that year, racial tensions were on the rise after a number of provocations by both whites and blacks. The increasing violence eventually erupted into riots during which the black section of the city was stormed on 1 June 1921. Dozens were killed, mainly blacks, and many buildings owned by blacks were burned down. Some sources have claimed that these fires were actually started by police officers who had commandeered private planes and used them to drop dynamite upon the segregated black communities.

**www.aerospaceweb.org/question/history/q0118.shtml**
$200,000 in 2017 -
**www.dollartimes.com/inflation/inflation.php?amount=200000&year=1921**

85. Carter G. Woodson – Historian (1875–1950), Carter G. Woodson was an African-American writer and historian known as the "Father of Black

History Month." He penned the influential book The Mis-Education of the Negro.

Carter Godwin Woodson was born on December 19, 1875, in New Canton, Virginia, to Anna Eliza Riddle Woodson and James Woodson. The fourth of seven children, young Woodson worked as a sharecropper and a miner to help his family. He began high school in his late teens and proved to be an excellent student, completing a four-year course of study in less than two years.

After attending Berea College in Kentucky, Woodson worked for the U.S. government as an education superintendent in the Philippines and undertook more travels before returning to the U.S. Woodson then earned his bachelor's and master's from the University of Chicago and went on to receive a doctorate from Harvard University in 1912—becoming the second African American to earn a Ph.D. from the prestigious institution, after W.E.B. Du Bois. After finishing his education, Woodson dedicated himself to the field of African-American history, working to make sure that the subject was taught in schools and studied by scholars. For his efforts, Woodson is often called the "Father of Black History."

In 1915, Carter G. Woodson helped found the Association for the Study of Negro Life and History (which later became the Association for the Study of Afro-American Life and History), which had the goal of placing African-American historical contributions front and center. The next year he established the Journal of Negro History, a scholarly publication.

Woodson also formed the African-American-owned Associated Publishers Press in 1921 and would go on to write more than a dozen books over the years, including A Century of Negro Migration (1918), The History of the Negro Church (1921), The Negro in Our History (1922) and Mis-Education of the Negro (1933). Mis-Education—with its focus on the Western indoctrination system and African-American self-empowerment—is a particularly noted work and has become regularly course adopted by college institutions.

In addition to his writing pursuits, Woodson also worked in a number of educational positions, serving as a principal for Washington, D.C.'s Armstrong Manual Training School before working as a college dean at Howard University and the West Virginia Collegiate Institute.

Woodson lobbied schools and organizations to participate in a special program to encourage the study of African-American history, which began in February 1926 with Negro History Week. The program was later expanded and renamed Black History Month. (Woodson had chosen February for the initial weeklong celebration to honor the birth months of abolitionist Frederick Douglass and President Abraham Lincoln.)

To help teachers with African-American studies, Woodson later created the Negro History Bulletin in 1937 and also penned literature for elementary and secondary school students.

Woodson died on April 3, 1950, a respected and honored figure who received accolades for his vision. His legacy continues on, with Black History Month being a national cultural force recognized by a variety of media formats, organizations and educational institutions.

**www.biography.com/people/carter-g-woodson-9536515**

For Carter G Woodson's full Biography see:
**www.blackpast.org/aah/woodson-carter-g-1875-1950**

86. Ajala, Godwin O. (1968–2001) is remembered as a U.S. national hero who fought to save the lives of countless people as they escaped from the World Trade Center Towers on September 11, 2001. He is also the only Nigerian listed among the nearly 3,000 people who died because of the attack.

    For Godwin Ajala's Full Biography see: **www.blackpast.org/gah/ajala-godwin-o-1968-2001**

87. The Mossi were a highly feudal society of horse warriors who founded several kingdoms on the steppe-like high plateau of the Upper Volta river basin, becoming feared enemies of the neighbouring Mali and Songhai Empires. Today, the Mossi number approximately 2.2 million people, representing approximately one third of the current population of Burkina Faso.

    The Mossi were not indigenous to the region, but migrated with their horses, assimilating the local tribes, and coalescing from clans into several kingdoms over time. Oral tradition and ethnological research offer several points of proposed origin in central and eastern Africa, and also places their primary migration anywhere between the 11th-15th century. One theory connects the Mossi with the African kingdoms of Dagomba, Gonja, and Mamprusi in the south. Whatever their origin, from early accounts in Songhai, it appears that the Mossi were well-established raiders as early as 1260 AD.

The Mossi's own founding myth, handed down through the ages, goes somewhat as follows: Forty generations ago, a king named Naba Nedega of Dagomba had a warrior daughter named Princess Nyennega, whom he would not allow to marry. Princess Nyennega struck out on horseback riding to the north, where she met and married a local man of the Bisa (or Mande) people. Their son, named Ouedraogo (stallion), was sent to be raised by his grandfather, Naba Nedega. When he grew up, he returned to the north with cavalry and conquered his father's people. The marriage of Ouedraogo and his troops with Bisa women produced the Mossi people. A statue of Princess Nyennega in the city of Ouagadougou commemorates the story.

Within the Volta basin, the Mossi coalesced into five independent kingdoms - Tenkodogo, Yatenga, Gourma, Zandoma, and Ouagadougou— each ruled by a king or naba. Ouagadougou emerged as the most powerful of the kingdoms, surviving to the present day as the capital city of Burkina Faso and home to the present-day King, whose powers are largely ceremonial.
Mossi (1250-1575 AD):
**www.fanaticus.org/DBA/armies/Variants/mossi.html**

88. Nielsen Report: "Black Girl Magic" And Brand Loyalty Is Propelling Total Black Buying Power Toward $1.5 Trillion By 2021:
**www.nielsen.com/us/en/press-room/2017/nielsen-report-black-girl-magic-and-brand-loyalty-is-propelling-black-buying-power.html**

89. Val McCalla (3 October 1943 in Kingston, Jamaica – 22 August 2002 in Seaford, East Sussex) is best known as the founder of The Voice, a British weekly newspaper aimed at the Britain's black community. He founded it in 1982 as a voice for the British African-Caribbean community. He was honoured as a pioneering publisher for the community, but also faced critics who deemed him sensationalistic. In the 100 Great Black Britons poll conducted in 1997, Val McCalla was voted number 68.

After studying accountancy at Kingston College in Jamaica, McCalla arrived in England in May 1959, aged 15. He joined the RAF, leaving in the mid-1960s. He was employed in various accounts and book-keeping positions, before working part-time on a community newspaper, East End News, based near his flat in Bethnal Green. He started The Voice newspaper in 1982, launching it at the Notting Hill carnival that August. Val McCalla died on 22 August 2002 of liver failure.

**https://en.wikipedia.org/wiki/Val_McCalla**

For Val McCalla's full Biography and 100 Great Black Britons Ranking see: **www.100greatblackbritons.com/bios/val_mccalla.html**

90. Sojourner Truth, born Isabella ("Belle") Baumfree; c. 1797 – November 26, 1883) was an African-American abolitionist and women's rights activist. Truth was born into slavery in Swartekill, Ulster County, New York, but escaped with her infant daughter to freedom in 1826. After going to court to recover her son, in 1828 she became the first black woman to win such a case against a white man.
She gave herself the name Sojourner Truth in 1843 after she became convinced that God had called her to leave the city and go into the countryside "testifying the hope that was in her." Her best-known speech was delivered extemporaneously, in 1851, at the Ohio Women's Rights Convention in Akron, Ohio. The speech became widely known during the Civil War by the title "Ain't I a Woman?," a variation of the original speech re-written by someone else using a stereotypical Southern dialect; whereas Sojourner Truth was from New York and grew up speaking Dutch as her first language. During the Civil War, Truth helped recruit black troops for the Union Army; after the war, she tried unsuccessfully to secure land grants from the federal government for former slaves.

**The Norton Anthology of African American Literature, 3rd Edition, Vol 1**
**https://en.wikipedia.org/wiki/Sojourner_Truth**

Truth started dictating her memoirs to her friend Olive Gilbert, and in 1850 William Lloyd Garrison privately published her book, The Narrative of Sojourner Truth: A Northern Slave.

"Women In History - Sojourner Truth". Women in History Ohio. February 27, 2013

91. The Black Panther Party or the BPP (originally the Black Panther Party for Self-Defense) was a revolutionary black nationalist and socialist organization founded by Bobby Seale and Huey Newton in October 1966. The party was active in the United States from 1966 until 1982, with international chapters operating in the United Kingdom in the early 1970s. and in Algeria from 1969 until 1972.

Federal Bureau of Investigation Director J. Edgar Hoover called the party "the greatest threat to the internal security of the country"
**"Hoover Calls Panthers Top Threat to Security". The Washington Post. WP Company LLC d/b/a The Washington Post. 16 July 1969.**

The BPP originated in Oakland, California, by founders Huey Newton and Bobby Seale. The Original six members of the Black Panthers included Elbert "Big Man" Howard, Sherman Forte, Reggie Forte, Little Bobby Hutton, and Newton and Seale. They adopted the Black Panther symbol from an independent political party established the previous year by Black residents of Lowndes County, Alabama. The Panthers also supported the Black Power movement, which stressed racial dignity and self-reliance.
**www.aaregistry.org/historic_events/view/black-panther-party-founded**

The Black Panthers Party launched the Free Breakfast For Children program: The party saw a serious need to nurture black kids in disenfranchised communities, so they spent about two hours each morning cooking breakfast for children in poor neighborhoods before school. "Studies came out saying that children who didn't have a good breakfast in the morning were less attentive in school and less inclined to do well and suffered from fatigue," former party member David Lemieux said in the documentary. "We just simply took that information and a program was developed to serve breakfast to children," he added. "We were showing love for our people." The party served about 20,000 meals a week and it became the party's most successful program of their 35 survival programs.

**www.huffingtonpost.com/entry/27-important-facts-everyone-should-know-about-the-black-panthers_us_56c4d853e4b08ffac1276462**

92. Age 60 marital status Divorced, 2 children, 1 divorce Hometown Washington, DC, United States. Education University of Illinois, Bachelor of Arts / Science. Princeton University, Master of Arts. Founder of Black Entertainment Television became nation's first African-American billionaire in 2001 by selling cable channel to Viacom for $3 billion. Ex-wife, Sheila, took big chunk the following year in divorce. Rebuilding fortune with hotel investments: bought 100 hotels for $1.7 billion from Dean White (see) in August. Also became first person of colour to hold a controlling interest in a professional sports team: owns basketball's Charlotte Bobcats. Other investments: recording studios (Three Keys Music), restaurants (Posh).
**https://www.forbes.com/lists/2006/54/biz_06rich400_Robert-L-Johnson_VYCO.html**

93. Mikaila Ulmer's Official Website – 'Our Story' provides an overview of how 'Me & The Bee's' was created.

    **www.meandthebees.com/pages/about-us**

    11-year-old entrepreneur lands multi-million deal with Whole Foods to sell her homemade lemonade:
    **www.telegraph.co.uk/news/2016/03/31/11-year-old-entrepreneur-lands-multi-million-deal-with-whole-foo/**

94. Maggie Lena Walker (July 15, 1864 – December 15, 1934) was an African-American teacher and businesswoman. Walker was the first female bank president of any race to charter a bank in the United States.

    **Alan Brinkley, "Chapter 15: Reconstruction and the New South". Edited by Emily Barrosse, American History, A Survey, Los Angeles, CA: McGraw Hill, p. 425.**

95. Suzanne Shank is President and CEO of Siebert Cisneros Shank & Co., LLC. In 1996, she founded the firm alongside Wall Street legend Muriel 'Mickie' Siebert. She is also the majority owner of the firm. Suzanne is considered the most powerful woman on the Wall Street right now. She is the first African-American woman in history to lead a publicly traded organization. She became more famous in 2013 when she was made the acting CEO of

the Siebert Financial Corporation. Suzanne has won several awards during her career. She is considered a finance maven. The estimated net worth of Suzanne Shank is not made public yet.

Suzanne Shank got her first job on Wall Street in 1987. She joined a small firm because she felt more comfortable there. She was taught to be hard working from her parents and had a firm belief of things going her way eventually. She co-founded 'Siebert Cisneros Shank & Co., LLC' in 1996 and has been its President and CEO since.

After becoming the acting CEO of Siebert Financial Corporation in 2013, she now holds two of the most powerful Wall Street companies. During her tenure as a CEO, Siebert Cisneros Shank has completed over $2 trillion of transactions for state and local authorities. Before starting a career in financial services, Suzanne took a job as Structural Engineering at General Dynamics.

Suzanne Shank has been awarded numerous awards throughout her career. She has been listed in 'Top 25 Women in Finance' by Essence Magazine in their Power List. She was also named one of the 'Top 100 Women in 2016' by Crain's Detroit Business.
**https://thenetworthportal.com/celeb-net-worth/businessperson/suzanne-shank-net-worth/**

96. Akon Provides Electricity To 80 Million Africans: Here in the west, Akon is a celebrity mostly known by his musical hits like "Locked Up," "Lonely," "Belly Dancer," and "Ghetto" to name just a few. But his most amazing noteworthy achievement and legacy, which has not been mentioned much in the mainstream western media, is that through his entrepreneurial endeavors stemming from the success that he had through his music career, he has changed the fate and quality of life of millions of Africans through his Akon Lights Africa Project.

Akon sidestepped the political challenges and roadblocks stemming from the oil industry by partnering with a Chinese solar power manufacturer and founding a renewable solar powered energy company that is currently providing electricity to approximately 16 million Africans in 15 countries, and this number continues to rise everyday.

By late 2017, it is estimated that Akon Lights Africa will be providing electricity to 80 million Africans. There are currently 600 million Africans in remote areas who have no access to electricity.

Akon's company is the fastest growing solar powered electricity provider in the world. His efforts and contribution to the African people are undeniably astonishing, staggering, and game-changing. His project is profoundly influencing the future of Africa and through this example, clearly setting the stage for the shifts to come to our energy infrastructures.

Full Story Available at: **www.collective-evolution.com/2016/08/29/akon-provides-electricity-to-80-million-africans/**

97. The Story of Wall Street's First Black Millionaire: Jeremiah Hamilton made white clients do his bidding. He bought insurance policies on ships he purposely destroyed. And in 1875, he died the richest black American.

    Jeremiah G. Hamilton. As an African American broker in the mid-1800s, Hamilton was part of no one's usable past: Wall Street in that time was completely white, and New York's black leaders disdained him for his brashness.

    But his death, in 1875, attracted national attention, and scores of newspapers reported that Hamilton was the richest non-white man in the country and that his estate was worth about $2 million.

    Hamilton worked in and around Wall Street for 40 years. Far from being some novice feeling his way around the economy's periphery, he was a skilled and innovative financial manipulator.

    **www.theatlantic.com/business/archive/2015/10/wall-street-first-black-millionaire/411622/**

    $2,000,000 in 1875 → $43,194,988.53 in 2017
    **www.in2013dollars.com/1875-dollars-in-2017?amount=2000000**

98. Madam C.J. Walker, Entrepreneur, Civil Rights Activist, Philanthropist (1867–1919). Madam C.J. Walker, born Sarah Breedlove, created specialized hair products for African-American hair and was one of the first American women to become a self-made millionaire.

After suffering from a scalp ailment that resulted in her own hair loss, she invented a line of African-American hair care products in 1905. She promoted her products by traveling around the country giving lecture-demonstrations and eventually established Madame C.J. Walker Laboratories to manufacture cosmetics and train sales beauticians. By the time she died, at 51, it was impossible to dismiss Walker. A generous philanthropist, she donated to scholarship funds, the NAACP, and campaigns to stop lynching. She helped to build a black YMCA in Indianapolis and restore Frederick Douglass's home in Washington.

"At a time when unskilled white workers earned about $11 a week, Walker's agents were making $5 to $15 a day, pioneering a system of multilevel marketing that Walker and her associates perfected for the black market," wrote Harvard professor Henry Louis Gates Jr. in a 1998 story for TIME.

http://time.com/3641122/sarah-breedlove-walker/

99. There are 2,043 people across the globe with three commas in their net worths, according to the 2017 Forbes Billionaires list. The 23 wealthiest have $1 trillion collectively.

In 2017, 10 of the world's billionaires — fewer than 1% — are black, down from 12 last year, reports Forbes contributor Mfonobong Nsehe. Three of the 10 are women. All but one, Isabel Dos Santos, are billed by Forbes as self-made.

To compile the full list, Forbes uses stock prices and exchange rates to estimate the net worths of the world's richest people, and then ranks them based on their wealth. This year's list was created using data from February 17, 2017, but Forbes also maintains a current snapshot of the world's billionaires, updated daily.

For each of the mentioned profiles see:
http://uk.businessinsider.com/black-billionaires-list-forbes/#mohammed-ibrahim-114-billion-1

For Real-time ranking see:
www.forbes.com/billionaires/list/20/#version:realtime

100. There African-American Women: Our Science, Her Magic:
     **www.nielsen.com/us/en/insights/reports/2017/african-american-women-our-science-her-magic.html /**

And this has most especially not been the case among firms owned by women of color – their numbers have more than doubled since 2007, increasing by 126%. In fact, there are nearly 2.8 million more firms owned by women of color now than in 2007, among an overall increase of 3.5 million in the number of women-owned firms. This means that nearly eight out of every 10 (79%) net new women-owned firms launched since 2007 has been started by a woman of color.

As of 2016, there are an estimated 1.9 million African American women-owned firms, employing 376,500 workers and generating $51.4 billion in revenues. Between 2007 and 2016, the number of African American women-owned firms increased by 112% - more than doubling in number and far out shadowing the overall 45% increase among all women-owned firms. African American women-owned firms constitute a 61% majority of African American-owned firms.

What's more, the 2016 State of Women-Owned Businesses Report found that whilst women now own 38 percent of all businesses in the United States, 44 percent of those women-owned firms are owned by minority women. Those owned by black women in particular employ around 376,500 workers and generate $51.4 billion in revenue.

# Picture Credits:

- J. A. Rogers – Public Domain.
- Jean Michel Basquiats – www.basquiat.com / www.sothebys.com/en/news-video/blogs/all-blogs/contemporary/2017/04/monumetnal-basquiat-leads-contemporary-art-evening-sale.html
- Frank Yerby - Wikipedia
- Chaka Khan – Essence Magazine
- Wooden statue of the visor Ptah-Hotep in the Imhotep Museum in Saqqara
- Sudan Pyramids - www.corespirit.com
- Ramani Wilfred - Daily Mirror
- Dorothy Vaughan, Mary Jackson, and Katherine Johnson - www.essence.com
- Dr. Mae C. Jeminson – NASA
- Ernie Davies – Getty Images
- Ademola Odujinrin - www.thenationonlineng.net
- Author Zang - Marc Arthur Zang Facebook account.
- Dr Shirley Jackson - Rensselaer Polytechnic Institute (RPI) Official Website
- Ludwick Marishane - Tshepo Kekana.
- Henrietta Lacks - shuttershack
- Plates vi & vii of the Edwin Smith Papyrus - New York Academy of Medicine
- Bernie Grant – The Voice
- Samora Moisés Machel – Public Domain
- Teytul Betul – Public Domain
- Thomas Sankara - ThomasSankara.net
- Kwame Nkrumah - www.britannica.com
- Patrice Lumumba - www.britannica.com
- Usain Bolt – Reuters
- Pele - Public Domain
- Simone Biles - www.nbcolympics.com
- Carl Brashear - www.awesomestories.com
- Trevor Mcdonald – ITV
- Carter G Woodson – Public Domain
- First editor Flip Fraser, founder Val McCalla and deputy editor Sharon Ali – The Voice
- Boby Seale & Huey Newton – Public Domain
- Mikaila Ulmer - www.blackamazing.com
- Akon – David Monteford

## Back Cover

- Amenhotep III & Tiye @ Cairo Museum - @Omega_Axsal
- Chief - Ghanaian chief with his Royal family - Mark Gellineau
- Kaepernick – Getty Images

## Patreon

Peace & More Powers family, thank you for getting involved and supporting the book. I would appreciate your time in taking a look at my Patreon account. Patreon is a platform that allows me to create culturally historic & spiritually educational content for subscribers all across the world to help aid and improve their studies on their pursuit for self-mastery.

My main focus is to research show and share culturally historic information to reconnect black African people of the diaspora back to their ancestral roots. I specialise particularly in ancient Kemite and Kushite history with three trips to the Nile Valley. As black people, we have been stripped of our history a great leader within our community we should all know Marcus Garvey said "a people with no knowledge of history and culture is like a tree with no roots."

So, this platform allows me to share with you the results of my research in the form of presentations, blog posts and live streams directly to your smartphone or tablet. Everyone who subscribes receives monthly benefits such as free ebooks, free access to events, exclusive content, discounts and the ability to help me contribute to projects rebuilding the African community that need our attention.

www.Patreon.com/UneferAxsal

www.Instagram.com/Omega_Axsal / www.Instagram.com/YUSALIFE

www.Twitter.com/OmegaAxsal / www.Twitter.com/YUSALIFE

If you'd like to invite me to speak or present at your event or would like an event in your area please reach out via email.

Axsal@YUSAbundance.com

## Origins of Black Excellence British Museum Tour

Since late 2016, after 4 years research and countless field trips to the British Museum in central London, I have been running the Black Excellence Museum tour guiding our brothers and sisters around the 6 Nile valley dedicated rooms. It's said that history favours those that control the narrative and for too long a distorted Eurocentric filter has been applied to the continent of Africa, the descendants across the diaspora and the continuous and never-ending input to the evolution of the world.

The reality of the situation is Black African people are the original standard of excellence and the lies told to disconnect black African people from the greatness are losing their effectiveness because we can now see, explore and study for ourselves what was left for us in the stone.

If you're local, or ever in London, join me at the British Museum the home of the largest collection of Kemetic artefacts outside of Kemet (present day Egypt) and take a step back in time to explore the origins of advanced civilisation and witness for yourself what the ancestors left behind.

I'll guide you through the dedicated rooms containing over 100,000 artefacts coving a provable 6000 years minimum of unbroken culture. See first-hand the sheer magnificence and be amongst the vibration of timeless brilliance whilst learning about the life and perspective of the ancient Kemetau.

 You'll leave having seen the mummies, statues, artwork, steles including the Rosetta stone and countless other evidences that will prove to you once and for all Africa is the birth place of excellence.

All children under 16s attend for free and every receives an inclusive PDF study guide to maximise your time at the museum and your future studies! Footage from previous tours in available via my social media and Patreon account.

## Did You Know?

You're not just supporting me by purchasing this book! And, you're not just improving things for yourself by learning from this book becase for every copy sold online via amazon 50% of the profits will be donated to the on-going projects and works conducted in the efforts to improve the quality of life, education and health of our brothers and sisters across the world.

Many of the projects will be continental based such as the Orphanage project conducted and maintained by Chaka Clarke (@Chakabars) in Kinshasa of the Democratic Republic of the Congo. Many children are abandoned, impoverished and left with very little chance of survival in extreme areas which is why projects like this need our attention and why I'm happy to support however I can.

### www. GoFundMe.com/UniteForTheChildren

One of the major projects which will be supported by the sales of this publication is the #WeWillRizeTogether project headed by Chronix, Fused ODG and Chakabars.

A mighty efford is made to disassociate the Caribbean islands with the west coast of Africa and for many years great people such as Marcus Garvey, Thomas Sankara and Kwame Nkrumah have attempted to oppose the white supremacist agenda to reunite black African people of the Caribbean to their ancestral roots.

Chronix & Fuse both have schools in their respective homelands (Jamaica and Ghana) and the plan is to improve them through refurbishment and create a volunteering program around the schools so we can build up the communities offering long-term opportunities.

The larger plan is to unite Jamaican & West African people at all levels from politicians, entertainers and sportsmen down to the very people that power villages, towns and cities so that we can break down the international barriers and reunite to improve the overall condition of melanated people across the world and spark the next Golden Age of the African.

### www.GoFundMe.com/WeWillRizeTogether

## J. A. Rogers Works.

Joel managed to publish 39 works, which in their totality alongside his physical presence played a tremendously positive role in educating, empowering and uplifting the diaspora:

1. From "Superman" to Man.
2. As Nature Leads.
3. The Approaching Storm and Bow it May be Averted: An Open Letter to Congress.
4. Music and Poetry: The Noblest Arts, Music and Poetry, vol. 1.
5. The Thrilling Story of The Maroons.
6. The West Indies: Their Political, Social, and Economic Condition.
7. Blood Money.
8. The Ku Klux Klan A Menace or A Promise.
9. Jazz at Home.
10. What Are We, Negroes or Americans?
11. Book Review, Jazz, by Paul Whiteman. Opportunity: A Journal of Negro Life, Volume 4, Number 48.
12. The Negro's Experience of Christianity and Islam.
13. The American Occupation of Haiti: Its Moral and Economic Benefit.
14. The Negro in Europe.
15. The Negro in European History.
16. World's Greatest Men of African Descent.
17. The Americans in Ethiopia," under the pseudonym Jerrold Robbins.
18. Enrique Diaz.
19. 100 Amazing facts about the Negro with Complete Proof. A Short Cut to the World History of the Negro.
20. World's Greatest Men and Women of African Descent.
21. Italy Over Abyssinia.
22. The Real Facts About Ethiopia.
23. When I Was In Europe.
24. Hitler and the Negro.
25. The Suppression of Negro History.
26. Your History: From the Beginning of Time to the Present.
27. An Appeal From Pioneer Negroes of the World, Inc: An Open Letter to His Holiness Pope Pius XII.
28. Sex and Race: Negro-Caucasian Mixing in All Ages and All Lands, Volume I: The Old World.
29. Sex and Race: A History of White, Negro, and Indian Miscegenation in the Two Americas, Volume II: The New World

30. Sex and Race, Volume III: Why White and Black Mix in Spite of Opposition.
31. World's Great Men of Color, Volume I.
32. World's Great Men of Color, Volume II.
33. Jim Crow Hunt.
34. Nature Knows No Color Line: Research into the Negro Ancestry in the White Race.
35. Facts About the Negro 2$^{nd}$ Edition.
36. Africa's Gift to America: The Afro-American in the Making and Saving of the United States. With New Supplement Africa and its Potentialities.
37. She Walks in Beauty.
38. "Civil War Centennial: Myth and Reality", Freedomways, vol. 3, no. 1
39. The Five Negro presidents: According to What White People Said They Were.

**Source: https://en.wikipedia.org/wiki/Joel_Augustus_Rogers#Works**

# 100 Recommended Reads.

For the real Knowledge Monsters hungry for that information, a recommended reading list in no particular order!

1. The Golden Age of West African Civilization - Raphael Ernest Grail Armattoe
2. Stole Legacy - George G. M. James
3. The Destruction of Black Civilisation - Chancellor Williams
4. The Rebirth of Black Civilisation - Chancellor Williams
5. When We Ruled – Robin Walker
6. They Came Before Columbus – Dr. Ivan Van Sertima
7. The Golden Age of the Moor – Dr. Ivan Van Sertima
8. African Presence in Early Europe – Dr. Ivan Van Sertima
9. Black Women in Antiquity, 2nd Edition – Dr. Ivan Van Sertima
10. Blacks in Science: Ancient and Modern – Dr. Ivan Van Sertima
11. Pagan Origins of the Christ Myth – John G Jackson
12. Christianity Before Christ – John G Jackson
13. The Golden Ages of Africa – John G Jackson
14. Man, God, & Civilization – John G Jackson
15. Africans at the Crossroads: African World Revolution - John Henrik Clarke
16. Christopher Columbus and the Afrikan Holocaust: Slavery and the Rise of European Capitalism - John Henrik Clarke
17. Who Betrayed the African World Revolution? - John Henrik Clarke
18. Cheikh Anta Diop And the New Light on African History - John Henrik Clarke
19. My Life in Search of Africa - John Henrik Clarke
20. Notes For An African World Revolution - John Henrik Clarke
21. Africa Mother of Western Civilization – Dr. Yosef ben-Jochannan
22. African Origins of the Major Western Religions – Dr. Yosef ben-Jochannan
23. Black Man of the Nile – Dr. Yosef ben-Jochannan
24. Cultural Genocide In The Black And African Studies Curriculum – Dr. Yosef ben-Jochannan
25. Blueprint for Black Power: A Moral, Political, and Economic Imperative for the Twenty-First Century – Dr. Amos Wilson
26. Developmental Psychology of the Black Child – Dr. Amos Wilson
27. Awakening the Natural Genius of Black Children – Dr. Amos Wilson
28. Afrikan Centered Consciousness Versus the New World Order: Garveyism in the Age of Globalism – Dr. Amos Wilson
29. The Isis Papers: The Keys to the Colours – Dr. Frances Cress Welsing
30. The Mis-Education of the Negro – Carter G. Woodson
31. African Myths and Folk Tales – Carter G. Woodson
32. The Souls of Black Folk – W. E. B. Du Bois
33. The World and Africa: An Inquiry into the Part which Africa has Played in World History – W. E. B. Du Bois
34. Interesting Narrative of The Life Of Olaudah Equiano - Olaudah Equiano / Gustavus Vassa

35. How Europe Underdeveloped Africa – Walter Rodney
36. The YUSA Guide to Balance: Mind Body Spirit – YUSALIFE
37. Intellectual Warfare – Jacob H Carruthers, PhD
38. MDW NTR Divine Speech: A Historiographical Reflection of African Deep Thought – Jacob H Carruthers, PhD
39. The Irritated Genie - Jacob H. Carruthers
40. African Kingdoms Hardcover – Basil Davidson
41. The African Slave Trade Paperback – Basil Davidson
42. Medu Ntr Volume 1,2,3,4 & 5 – By Ra Un Amen Nefer
43. African Glory Paperback – J. C. Degraft- Johnson
44. Exiled Egyptians – Mustapha Gadalla
45. Spiritual Warriors are Healers – Mfundishi Jhutymus
46. Seven White Lies – Mr. Jabari G Osaze
47. Wonderful Ethiopians of the Ancient Cushite Empire – Drusilla Dunjee Houston
48. Per M Heru - The Book of Enlightenment - Muata Ashby
49. The Kemetic Tree of Life Ancient Egyptian Metaphysics and Cosmology for Higher Consciousness – Muata Ashby
50. African Origins: African Origins of African Civilization, Religion, Yoga Spirituality and Ethics Philosophy – Muata Ashby
51. The African Origin of Civilization: Myth or Reality? – Cheikh Anta Diop
52. Precolonial Black Africa – Cheikh Anta Diop
53. Civilization or Barbarism – Cheikh Anta Diop
54. Medical Apartheid: The Dark History of Medical Experimentation – Harriet A. Washington
55. Afrikan Holistic Health – Dr. Lliala Afrika
56. Afrikan Genesis, Vol. 1 Paperback – Ishakamusa Barashango
57. Afrikan People and European Holidays, Vol.1: A Mental Genocide – Ishakamusa Barashango
58. Echoes of the Old Darkland: Themes from the African Eden Paperback – Charles S. Finch III
59. Pillars in Ethiopian History – William Leo Hansberry
60. Africa and Africans as Seen by Classical Writers – William Leo Hansberry
61. History of Ancient Egypt – Erik Hornung
62. Wonderful Ethiopians of the Ancient Cushite Empire – Drusilla Dunjee Houston
63. What They Never Told You in History Class, Volume 1 – Indus Khamit-Kush
64. Introduction to Black Studies Paperback – Maulana Karenga
65. Ancient and Modern Britons (Volume 1) – David Macritchie
66. Ancient Egypt The Light of the World: Vol. 1 and 2 – Gerald Massey
67. The African Origin of Greek Philosophy: An Exercise in Afrocentrism Paperback – Innocent C. Onyewuenyi
68. Africa in the Iron Age c.500 B.C. to A.D.1400: C.500 BC-1400 AD Paperback – Roland Oliver
69. The Bornu Sahara and Sudan – Richard Sir Palmer
70. In Praise of Black Women: Ancient African Queens v. 1 – Simone Schwarz-Bart

71. In Praise of Black Women: Heroines of the Slavery Era v. 2 – Simone Schwarz-Bart
72. In Praise of Black Women: Modern African Women v. 3 – Simone Schwarz-Bart
73. A History of Islam in West Africa – J.Spencer Trimingham
74. General History of Africa volume 1: Methodology and African Prehistory – J. Ki-Zerbo
75. General History of Africa volume 2: Methodology and African Prehistory – G. Mokhtar
76. General History of Africa volume 3: Methodology and African Prehistory – I. Hrbek
77. General History of Africa volume 4. Africa from the 12th to the 16th Century – M. El Fasi
78. From Columbus to Castro: History of the Caribbean, 1492-1969 Paperback – Eric Eustace Williams
79. Autobiography of Malcolm X – Alex Haley
80. Philosophy and Opinions of Marcus Garvey – Marcus Garvey
81. Selected Writings and Speeches of Marcus Garvey – Marcus Garvey
82. Black Skin, White Masks – Frantz Fanon
83. A Dying Colonialism – Frantz Fanon
84. Alienation and Freedom – Frantz Fanon
85. The Wretched of the Earth – Frantz Fanon
86. Toward the African Revolution: Political Essays – Frantz Fanon
87. The Iceman Inheritance – Michael Brady
88. Fingerprints of the Gods – Graham Hancock
89. Think and Grow Rich - Napoleon Hill
90. Who Moved My Cheese – Dr Spencer Johnson
91. The Four Agreements – Don Miguel Ruiz
92. The Alchemist – Paul Coelho
93. 1984 – George Orwell
94. Animal Farm – George Orwell
95. The Message of the Sphinx – Graham Hancock & Robert Bauval
96. Egyptian Tales – W.M.Petrie
97. The Histories – Herodotus
98. Israel's Debt to Egypt – Book by Edward Sugden
99. Colonialism: Norrie Macqueen
100. Maat, The Moral Ideal in Ancient Egypt: A Study in Classical Egypt – Maulana Karenga

## 10 Affirmations for Self-Love, Success & Satisfaction

Your life is a projection of your thoughts both conscious and subconscious if your life is not how you want it, start your day with these affirmations think, speak, feel and act it into existence.

**I AM** alive, greateful and blessed with my health. **I AM** enough and I will not conform to a standard that doesn't accept me.

**I AM** a King/Queen, committed to self-improvement, my ancestry is wrapped in excellence, **I AM** here for a reason and **I AM** the architect of my life free to create my own reality.

**I AM** divine, my body is my temple, I absorb the sun as it kisses my flesh, **I AM** gifted with melanin and **I AM** my brother and sisters Keeper.

**I AM** able to accept all that makes me human, **I AM** perfect in all my imperfections, I will learn from mistakes and everything I experience makes me stronger.

**I AM** in line with my higher-self, striving for the best and achieving my goals with ease. **I AM** Prosperous in every form within and without.

**I AM** content being under construction, perfecting my craft, **I AM** wisdom, full of creative energy and **I AM** kindness constantly seeking to add value where I can.

**I AM** emotionally balanced, mentally healthy and wealth is my natural birthright, **I AM** not required to work for equality

**I AM** not defined by my current situation, I will not engage in destructive behavior that does not forward myself, my family, my community and my people.

**I AM** self-respecting enough to surround myself with those that love, support and appreciate me as I do them. **I AM** able to remove myself from situations and relationships that are toxic or not for my greater good.

**I AM** love with myself unconditionally and deserve the same level of respect that I offer to the world.

# The mdw nTr – Basic Offering

The ancient hieroglyphic language of the ancient Kemetau (Egyptians) was called the mdw nTr (Medu Netchur) and is widley thought to be the oldest complete language. Mdw nTr was a pictographic language based on the sounds, sights, ideas, concepts and principles drawn from their native environments. This is why we see glyphs, of different birds, mammals, plants, humans, tools, weapons and so on. There were actually three versions of the mdw nTr which evolved along with the advancement of Kemet there's:

- mdw nTr – Ceremonial texts used to decorate the tombs, seen on spiritual papyri, steles, and coffins.
- Hieratic – For official, state, legal and business correspondence. Hieratic is thought to have developed as a shorthand to the mdw Ntr
- Demotic – Appears in the late period and was the common script.

Learning to read and write the mdw nTr requires time, attention and dedication to understanding total African history, culture and spirituality. It also helps to have a good memory, a lot of the texts that we have available to study are ceremonial texts and over the agreed 3000 years their traditions continued, there was very few drastic changes.

This means people who're able to recognise patterns will find it easier, there are very commonly repeated lines in the mdw nTr called offering formulas. Offering formulas are literally found all over Kemetic art from in the burial tombs, steles, kA doors, status, and papyri, and they were used to literally offer praise & thanks to a nTr (God/Deity) in return for eternal abundance. The most commonly used offering formula is worshiping Wesir/Ausar, the nTr of duAt (afterlife) and with the Kemetau having such a fascination and preoccupation with the process and notion of death, this formula was everywhere.

For more information on how to start learning to read and write the Ancient language of the Kemetau search for the works of Rhkty Amen, Mfundishi Jhutymus Ka En Heru, Jabari Osaze or you can visit and support my patreon platform where there are videos and resources available.

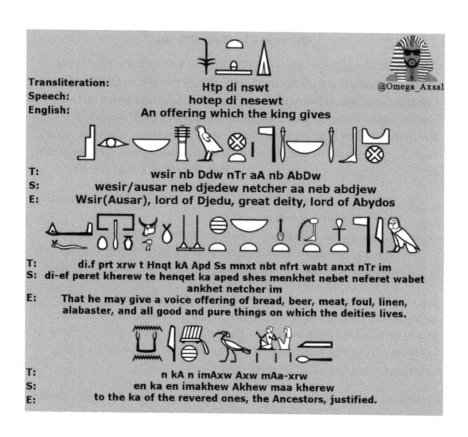

**Transliteration:** Htp di nswt
**Speech:** hotep di nesewt
**English:** An offering which the king gives

**T:** wsir nb Ddw nTr aA nb AbDw
**S:** wesir/ausar neb djedew netcher aa neb abdjew
**E:** Wsir(Ausar), lord of Djedu, great deity, lord of Abydos

**T:** di.f prt xrw t Hnqt kA Apd Ss mnxt nbt nfrt wabt anxt nTr im
**S:** di-ef peret kherew te henqet ka aped shes menkhet nebet neferet wabet ankhet netcher im
**E:** That he may give a voice offering of bread, beer, meat, foul, linen, alabaster, and all good and pure things on which the deities lives.

**T:** n kA n imAxw Axw mAa-xrw
**S:** en ka en imakhew Akhew maa kherew
**E:** to the ka of the revered ones, the Ancestors, justified.

## 10 Black Social Media Accounts

Here's 10 Pro-Black-African Instagram pages that will further your knowledge, keep you thinking and up to the times.

- @AncestorsWork
- @ChakaBars
- @CoupeDC
- @EmpressAK
- @Olmecian

- @TheRealBlackHistorian
- @DavidBanner
- @IAmHamamat
- @GhanaPosts
- @ThePanAfrican

## 10 Black Documentaries

- Slavery by Another Name
- Dark Girls
- Maafa 21: 21st Century Genocide
- The Black Wall Street
- Ethnic Notions

- Hidden Colours 1-4
- 13th
- Out of the Darkness
- 1804
- Life & Debt

## Lesson Plan

**#100DaysOfBlackExcellence**

To download the free and exclusive lesson plan, suitable for all ages simply send an email with your name, any feedback or images with the book to **AncestorsWork@yahoo.com** and the download will be to you within a few minutes.

The suggested guidelines provide an unimaginable amount of hours' worth of activities designed with raising critical thinkers in mind.

The free download also includes a set of free graphics which can be used as screensavers, social media posts and learn more about Black Brilliance.

**Ankh Udja Seneb**

**Life Prosperity & Health**

## Quiz Answers

## Initiate

- Sheffield, Westmoreland, Jamaica.
- The Piano.
- Chaka Khan.
- Mali
- Sudan
- IQ of 162
- Dr. Mae C. Jeminson
- Ghana
- Lemonade
- Carter G Woodson

## Initiated

- 39 total publications, From superman to man.
- Libya.
- 3000.
- Mohammad Baba.
- Dorothy Vaughan, Mary Jackson, and Katherine Johnson.
- Queen Philipa ruled 1328CE.
- Souljourner Truth.
- Democratic Republic of Congo.
- Suzanne Shank.
- Black Women.

## Illuminated

- Roger's covered the coronation of Emperor Hallie Selassie.
- The Association for the Study of Classical African Civilisations. Drs. John Henrik Clark, Asa Grant Hilliard, Leonard Jeffries, Jacob H. Carruthers, Rkhty Amen, Yosef Ben-Jochannan, and Maulana Karenga.
- Most profitable film of 2017.
- By urinating on sheets of emmer or barley
- Onesimus.
- Wrote the oldest complete book in the world.
- Inoculated 2.5 million children, improved the national literacy rate, increased farming yields, built schools and medical centres, fought against female genital mutilation.
- 18 including himself escaped on that ship that night.
- Black Wall Street.

Printed in the USA
CPSIA information can be obtained
at www.ICGtesting.com
LVHW022035081223
765941LV00015B/1625